SS–HITLERJUGEND

SS–HITLERJUGEND

THE HISTORY OF THE TWELFTH SS DIVISION 1943–45

Rupert Butler

SPELLMOUNT
Staplehurst

British Library Cataloguing in Publication Data:
A catalogue record for this book is available
from the British Library

Copyright © Amber Books Ltd 2003

ISBN 1-86227-193-3

First published in the UK in 2003 by
Spellmount Limited
The Old Rectory
Staplehurst
Kent TN12 0AZ

Tel: 01580 893730
Fax: 01580 893731
Email: enquiries@spellmount.com
Website: www.spellmount.com

Editorial and design by
Amber Books Ltd
Bradley's Close
74-77 White Lion Street
London N1 9PF
www.amberbooks.co.uk

Project Editor: Charles Catton
Editor: Caroline Curtis
Design: Neil Rigby at www.stylus-design.com
Picture Research: Lisa Wren

Printed and bound in Italy by: Eurolitho S.p.A., Cesano Boscone (MI)

The author would like to thank the Imperial War Museum,
the Institute of Contemporary History and Wiener Library, and the German Historical Institute,
all based in London, for research and assistance.

Picture credits

TRH Pictures: 6, 9, 10, 12–13, 14–15, 16, 17, 19, 20, 21, 22–23, 24–25, 26, 27, 32–33, 34–35, 37 (U.S. National Archives),
38, 40, 41, 42, 43, 44–45, 46, 52, 56, 64, 71, 82, 85, 96–97, 102–103, (U.S. Army) 106, 112–113, 116–117, 118, 119, 121,
128, 130–131, 139, 148–149, 156, 158–159, 160–161, 162–163, 164–165, 166–167, 169, 170, 172, 176, 178, 181 (Library
of Congress), 183;
Süddeutscher Verlag: 18, 28–29, 30, 48, 54, 55, 58–59, 68, 74, 78, 79, 89, 90, 101, 108–109, 114–115, 120, 122, 125,
126, 127, 132, 136–137, 144, 145, 146, 147, 150–151, 155, 168, 173;
Ian Baxter: 39, 47, 50–51, 53, 57, 60, 61, 62–63, 66, 70, 72–73, 75, 76, 77, 80–81, 86, 88, 93, 94, 99, 110, 134–135,
140, 142, 143, 152–153, 175;
Amber Books: 67, 94, 111, 119, 123;
Patrick Mulrey: 11, 38, 91.

Contents

CHAPTER ONE

BEGINNINGS

From the birth of his Nazi movement, Adolf Hitler set out to tap into
a promising source of recruits in the various groups and societies
associated with German youth. He appealed to the latent patriotism of a
generation anxious to build a new Germany from the ruins of the old.

Germany has a rich tradition of organizations for youth. Over the decades, there have been groups with a variety of beliefs and persuasions, including *Pfadfinder,* or boy scout, organizations that promoted little beyond good fellowship and camp fire camaradie. At the end of World War II, apologists for Nazi Germany tended to link the *Hitler Jugend,* or Hitler Youth, with the scouting fraternity, suggesting that its activities were largely confined to competitive sports and country rambles.

This was certainly a view that newsreels and the Nazi propaganda machine were keen to encourage. But this was only part of the story. Soon after securing power in 1933, Hitler announced his intention to create a state in which strict obedience and discipline were mandatory with the harshest penalties being reserved for dissenters. There was to be a very specific role for German youth, who were be mustered as instruments of war. The Führer's rousing call for a 'Thousand Year Reich' and his proclamation that, 'He alone who owns the youth gains the future', awoke a latent patriotism within the German people,

**Left: Adolf Hitler, as Chancellor, bows to President von
Hindenburg at a memorial service in Berlin in June 1934.
Immediately on Hindenburg's death Hitler merged the
offices of Chancellor and President to become *Der Führer*.**

who had till then been crippled by cynicism. A generation of youth was urging the rebirth of a Germany that had endured the twin fevers of political agitation and street violence during the Weimar Republic.

PATRIOTIC FERVOUR

At general mobilization in 1914, Germany had been gripped by a patriotic fervour and had faith in ultimate victory. In the Reichstag, differences had been set aside. Kaiser Wilhelm II, with his withered arm and imperial ambitions, had proclaimed triumphantly: 'I see no parties any more, only Germans.' By November, the German advance on the Western Front towards Paris had been halted on the Marne river. The German Fourth Army was given the order to cut through the defences that had been established by the Allies between Ypres and the Channel. The few regular soldiers in the Fourth Army were mainly young volunteers, many of them students and schoolboys who, with their last year at school remitted, had swarmed with enthusiasm to the colours. Typical of them was Walter Flex, a schoolteacher's son, who declared: 'We need a tough, hard-headed national idealism that is prepared for every sacrifice.'

Middle-class young men, impatient with politicians and theorists, believed firmly that victory in the war would be seized by them, rather than a fumbling older generation. Indeed, the potent idealism of Flex's contemporaries, who rejected the rhetoric of both Left and Right, had already led to the foundation of the German youth movement dedicated to freedom, embodied by the *Wandervogel*, or 'Birds of Passage', organization. Followers emphasized the rediscovery of nature, a rejection of materialism and an awareness of pre-industrial ways of life. Members were keen to adopt an individual, often rustic style of dress, and greeted one another with '*Heil*'.

The year before the outbreak of World War I saw the centenary of the Battle of the Nations at Leipzig, in which Prussian, Austrian and German forces had decisively beaten Napoleon. In commemoration, Kaiser Wilhelm II unveiled a monument at the scene of the fighting. The *Wandervogel* and other leagues of youth seized on the occasion to come together under the banner of the *Bündische Jugend*. A Festival of Youth was held on the evening of 11 October, when groups of boys and girls, including socialists and students from the nearby universities of Marburg, Göttingen and Jena, converged on a site at the Hohe Meissner, a mountain south of Kassel. The area was steeped in romantic legend; here, according to ancient folklore, lived Frau Holle, the legendary maker of snow. One speaker declared, 'The Free German Youth is determined to shape its own life, to be responsible to itself and guided by the innate feeling of truth. To defend this inner liberty, they close their ranks.'

With the outbreak of war in August 1914 came the belief that the conflict would sweep away the machinery of capitalist bureaucracy, together with the materialism so many of the *Wandervogel* despised. Disillusion was not long in coming. In Flanders, the XXVI Reserve Corps of the Fourth Army was sent into battle with orders to take the village of Langemarck, a heavily-defended strongpoint within the British position. The XXVI Reserve Corps, made up from young volunteers, was all but annihilated. To this day the visitor to the salient is faced with a cemetery containing 25,000 soldiers, buried together in a mass grave.

Above the chaos of battle at Langemarck, according to legend, an ardent voice could be heard intoning the future German national anthem, *Deutschland Lied, Deutschland über Alles*. The voice was taken up by others until there was mass singing amid the thunder of the English guns. While the stretcher bearers and the medics strove to remove the wounded and the dead, the singing could be heard across the battlefield, unceasing even while knots of survivors, clutching their rifles, returned to the action.

Whatever the truth of the legend, Langemarck served as useful propaganda, which the Nazis were quick to exploit when later sacrifices were required by German youth. The heady romanticism and youthful idealism that characterized the *Wandervogel* was coarsened by the sufferings of war. Within some of the youth groups, only praise for the virtues of peasant life survived intact.

Alongside those who strove to keep the ideals of the *Wandervogel* alive were such groups as the *Bündische Jugend*, whose followers looked back to the highlights of German military history, their factions adopting such titles as *Bismarck, Tannenberg, Hindenberg* or *Scharnhorst*. One of the most significant indications of the way in which such groups were developing was a widespread adoption of uniforms. These often took the form of shorts and a particular colour of shirt, whether white, blue, brown or grey. Distinctive headgear, notably the beret, was widely favoured and there were individual emblems and banners.

MUNICH PUTSCH

November 1923 saw Hitler, in a disastrous misjudgement, make a bid in Munich to seize power and overthrow the state government of Bavaria. The attempt ended in farce: Hitler was arrested and sentenced to five years' penal servitude, although he was released under amnesty within the year. During that time, 19-year-old Gustav Adolf Lenk was leader of the *Jugendbund,* an adjunct of the brown-shirted *Sturmabteilung* (Storm Troopers), or SA. Lenk was soon facing a rival, however.

Right: Members of the *Bismarck Jugend*, one of the youth groups which had always been on the political Right and which lost little time in proclaiming its alliance to Adolf Hitler after he became Chancellor in January 1933.

Kurt Gruber was a 20-year-old law student who had formed the *Grossdeutsche Jugendbewegung* (GDJB, Greater German Youth Movement). In an ensuing power struggle, Gruber emerged as the predominant force, his organization being recognized as the official youth movement of the National Socialist German Workers (Nazi) Party. During the course of the second *Reichsparteitag* (National Party Rally) at Weimar in July 1926, the GDJB was renamed *Hitler Jugend, Bund Deutscher Arbeiterjugend* (Hitler Youth, Union of German Worker Youth), inevitably shortened to *Hitler Jugend*. Gruber was appointed *Reichsführer* with responsibility for Youth Affairs throughout the whole of Germany and Austria.

Hitler, while careful to praise the endeavours of the Hitler Youth, was at the same time notoriously distrustful of any groups within his National Socialist organization that might pose even the remotest threat. To make sure Gruber's powers remained strictly limited, Hitler appointed a powerful corrective in *Hauptmann* Franz Felix Pfeffer von Salomon, a Prussian of Huguenot extraction and already a veteran Nazi. He had served in Westphalia as a member of the *Freikorps*, the private army of ex-soldiers that was raised at the end of World War I. More significantly, von Salomon had served as Chief of the SA and, as Hitler intended, the links with the Storm Troopers remained.

Left: Prescribed uniforms and insignia were slow to evolve in the early days of the *Hitler Jugend*, as this picture at an HJ rally on 1 May 1933 clearly shows. The distinctive HJ badge was yet to be adopted.

Below: The *Hitler Jugend* was organized on a regional basis. This map shows the various districts in 1938, after the *Anschluss* (union) with Austria and the absorption of the Sudetenland into the Greater German Reich.

The SA's most formidable presence was Ernst Röhm, the hardline professional soldier who considered his Storm Troopers to be the very essence of the Nazi revolution. By the end of 1931, the ranks of the SA's brown-shirted bully boys, addicted to intimida- tion and street violence, had been expanded to 170,000 men. This constituted the main force within the National Socialist Party, a truth that was recognized by another emerging member of the SA, Baldur von Schirach. To many, von Schirach's

made a good cheerleader at football games.' Von Schirach did indeed have American ancestry: his mother's side included two signatories to the Declaration of Independence and a grandfather who had been a Union officer and a casualty at the Battle of Bull Run. The record of his father was more appropriate: Carl Bailey-Norris von Schirach had been an officer in the *Garde-Kurassier* Regiment of Kaiser Wilhelm II.

Von Schirach edged himself into the exclusive circle of leading Nazis while at university in Munich, studying art history and German folklore. The higher reaches of the party certainly welcomed him for his organizational ability, but a talent for intrigue, allied with a specious charm, scarcely endeared him to the rough and ready street-fighting echelons of the Storm Troopers. Nor did he find a warm haven in the National Socialist Student Association, though he eventually succeeded in elbowing out its *Reichsführer,* Wilhelm Tempel.

STRUGGLE FOR POWER

Kurt Gruber, though, was a tougher proposition, and was not prepared to relinquish his power base without a struggle. In a bid to demonstrate that he was not von Salomon's creature, he won a concession that 18-year-old Hitler Youth members were no longer obliged to transfer to the SS. With some justification, Gruber could argue to Hitler that his achievements were considerable. From 80 branches in 1926, his movement had expanded by 1929 to around 450 branches, the membership having risen from 700 in 1926 to 13,000 in 1929.

None of this, however, was to the taste of Ernst Röhm, who lost no time in making it clear that he wanted even firmer control over the the Hitler Youth. Röhm's considerable influence over Hitler, together with von Schirach's close personal support, had its effect. A peremptory directive issued on 27 April 1931

antecedents seemed incongruous for high office under the Nazis. The celebrated American journalist and pre-war Berlin correspondent William Shirer wrote, 'Baldur von Schirach... looked rather like a sleek, shallow American college boy, the kind who

made it clear that Gruber would be directly subordinate to Röhm as Chief of Staff of the SA. What was more, Röhm was given the power of approving the appointment of senior members of the SA. The final humiliation was the instruction that Gruber relocate to Munich. He had made his headquarters in Plon in Saxony, where he was out of Röhm's easy reach; now he would have to endure the SA breathing down his neck.

RASH PROMISE

In response to a sneering comment from Röhm that the Hitler Youth could scarcely muster 25,000 followers, Gruber made the rash promise to double membership to 50,000 by the end of 1931. It was an impossible undertaking and the news from Munich headquarters of Gruber's 'resignation' was not long in coming. By any standards, it had been a squalid power battle. Hitler was anxious to divert attention from this, and swiftly published a new directive:

'Within the framework of the Supreme SA Command, a new office, *Reichsjugendführer*, has been created. The *Reichsjugendführer* is directly responsible to the Chief of Staff of the SA. To the post of *Reichsjugendführer* I appoint party member von Schirach... He keeps the Chief of Staff informed about all organizational problems of the youth formations with special emphasis on those affairs which involve the SA. His rank is that of a *Gruppenführer*, his uniform has yet to be determined.'

On 30 January 1933, Hitler had forged a successful alliance with the party of the Nationalists and the German Right, and was entrusted with the Chancellorship. Barely five months later, he gave von Schirach the new and more grandiose title of *Jugendführer des Deutschen Reiches* – Youth Leader of Germany. Von Schirach's new responsibilities included the authority to make sure that no new youth organization could be formed without his permission; it need hardly be said that he never gave it. The official

Left: *Reichjugendsführer* **Baldur von Schirach takes the salute at a march past of** *Hitler Jugend* **members. Marches and mass demonstrations became increasingly frequent during pre-war days under von Schirach's guidance.**

policy now was *Gleichstellung*. As far as the Hitler Youth was concerned, this meant not only the 'coordination' and 'integration' of all other other youth organizations, but also a total ban on such organizations. Those political associations whose organizers fondly believed they were exempt from the new ruling were quickly disabused.

It is at this point in the development of the Hitler Youth that the movement began to take on an even more militaristic complexion. The children of Nazi Germany were to become weapons of war, forged and tempered from the very moment of birth.

The Nazification of the German boy began even before he was eligible to join the *Deutsches Jungvolk,* a sort of preparatory school that led to membership of the Hitler Youth at 14. In the *Jungvolk,* he was a *Pimpf*

(Austrian term for 'shrimp'), receiving an education that had little in common with more conventional schools. A *Pimpf*'s initiation test, after which he received his first ceremonial dagger, consisted of learning and reciting key passages of Nazi dogma, together with verses from the *Horst Wessel Leid.* Before long, the infant head was expected to take in the rules of elementary war games, and the young child was also expected to take part in fund-raising. Innocence was quick to die; a story circulating among the parents of *Pimpfs* was about the mother of a

Below: The public view of the *Hitler Jugend* was of gatherings where everyone was united in good fellowship and camp fire camaraderie. It was an image that the Nazis were keen to foster.

ten-year-old who had asked him to play with the little girl next door, only to be told sharply, 'It's out of the question. I'm in uniform.'

Von Schirach went on to head the *Reichsjugend-führung*, an elephantine bureaucratic body that controlled a series of territorial commands, termed the *Obergebiet* and *Gebiet*. Originally, these commands corresponded to the 18 states of the German Reich, the largest being Prussia, which occupied more than half of Germany's total area. To accommodate densely populated regions, some of the territorial commands were subdivided into more simplified zones. For instance, the *Gebiet* of Saxony was structured into five *Obergebiet*, which were the main controlling

Above: The cultivation of physical fitness was a preoccupation of the *Hitler Jugend*. Competitive sporting events, such as this one attended by enthusiastic supporters during the early 1930s, were held frequently.

commands of the area. At the head of each chain of command was a *Gebietsführer*, a role combined with that of *Jungvolk Gebietsführer*, since his command extended to juniors. Then came the unit strengths within the *Hitler Jugend* and the *Jungvolk*, dominated by *Kameradschaft* which could include up to 15 boys. Units designated *Schar*, *Unterbann* and *Bann* (approximiating to Troops or Bands) and *Gefolgschaft* (Teams) were each in the care of an individual *Führer* (Leader).

Von Schirach's intention to convert each and every Hitler Youth member to accept the ethos of war reached its most spectacular expression on 20 April 1936, when Hitler was presented with a unique birthday present – every single boy and girl in the Reich who had been born in 1926 was invited to 'volunteer' to join the *Jungvolk,* the girls to be members of the *Jungmadel,* 'Young Maidens'.

This elaborate ceremony exhibited von Schirach's considerable flair for organization and stage management. The setting was the *Ordensburg* in Marienburg, East Prussia, close to the Polish frontier. It was an apposite choice since the *Ordensburgen* were the so-called 'Order Castles' of the Third Reich, recalling the activities of the Order of the Teutonic Knights of the 14th and 15th centuries. The knightly order was based on the principle of total obedience to the *Ordenmeister,* who decreed the German conquest of the Slavic lands and the enslavements of its peoples.

Above: The Nuremberg rally in 1936. The *Hitler Jugend* played a key role in these spectacular demonstrations of Nazi power. Speeches, marches, parades. flags and music were all geared to arouse frenetic support for Hitler.

For the *Jungvolk,* the group for children of ages 10 to 14, Marienburg was an experience that inspired awe. Amid the sombre light of candles and torches, the fledglings were to swear the oath that would be repeated on each subsequent 20 April, even as late in the war as 20 April 1945:

> I promise
> In the Hitler Youth
> To Do My Duty
> At all times
> In love and faithfulness
> To help the Führer
> So help me God

The oath-taking was orchestrated by fanfares of fifes and drum, including the refrain *'Vorwärts, vorwärts, schmettern die hellen Fanfaren'* – 'Forward, forward, the bright trumpets flare.' Progressively, the Hitler Youth movement took over the lives of its members. Over the weeks and months, parents, who believed at first that their sons were merely some sort of glorified boy scouts, swiftly realized their mistake. It was made clear that a child returning home was doing so on official leave, for a specified period. Bemused parents were confronted by their *Jungvolk* son proudly brandishing a knife resembling a *Wehrmacht* dagger, and wearing a uniform with *Jungvolk* insignia and the inevitable brown shirt. The ethos of the movement was exemplified by a booklet, *Deutsches Volk,* published in Halle. It featured a full page photograph of *Reichsjugendführer* von Schirach,

Below: The *Jungvolk* of the *Hitler Jugend*, its youngest members, some of whom are pictured here, were expected to play their full part in the gymnastic displays which were a highspot of the Nazi Party rallies.

below which was printed: 'Let us proclaim the purpose of our lives: the war has preserved us for the coming war'.

Then came a decree from Hitler that school was compulsory for five days a week, but Saturdays (at least) were reserved for the Hitler Youth. The Hitler Youth Camp in Munich was dominated by soaring, squat pylons topped by flaming beacons and giant swastikas. Here, on arrival, the boys could scarcely avoid seeing the giant hoarding with its stern injunction: *'Wir sind zu sterben fur Deutschland geboren'* – 'We are born to die for Germany.' The day began with a general flag parade at 7 a.m.

Beyond the guardhouse, sentry-post huts and khaki tents lay the sports area. Activities there were not intended merely to produce strong and healthy citizens, distinguished in the long jump or in the 100-yard relays. On the ground were long white lines, and while it is true that these resembled running tapes, any veteran of the trenches would have recognised their real purpose. They were of the kind pegged into the ground at night to guide troops to

breaches in front-line wire, to mortar and machine-gun assault positions.

A youth was also taught here how to outflank a machine gun post, how to take cover, and how to assemble at a position with maximum speed and minimum risk. In addition, there was an outdoor rifle range and an ordnance lecture theatre, its walls covered with map-reading charts and tactical diagrams. Tables were littered with guns and rifle components, shells and bullets. The weapons were stripped and bisected to display their working parts.

Two British journalists were invited to attend a similar camp at München-Gladbach in northwest Germany, where the emphasis on military training was obvious. One of the reporters wrote:

'Presently, a company of about 80 boys of 11 years of age arrived. They were in charge of a squadron leader aged 16. He was the most exacting martinet I have ever had the pleasure of meeting. He told us, with disgust in his voice, that although they had had many drill lessons they were still unable to march with military precision. Everyone was agreed on the enormity of this crime. Our martinet friend drilled his squad for a while, and then gave up in disgust. He informed us he would take them to see the military

Below: Even after a full week of conventional schooling, boys were obliged to devote at least one day of the weekend – if not both days – to *Hitler Jugend* activities, notably fitness and sports.

Above: Sporting activities within the *Hitler Jugend* were soon taking on a militaristic complexion, as Germany prepared for war. These youngsters are practising grenade-throwing with dummy weapons.

and some proper marching. We accompanied them to the military camp about a mile away. Three thousand soldiers were there, the first time since 1919. By six o'clock that night those little boys of 11 had achieved their leader's life-time ambition, they would march with military precision. There was a smile of happiness and contentment on their faces.'

'… A small boy knocked on the door on some errand or other. He was sent outside five times for not clicking his heels as he said "Heil Hitler" before beginning to speak to his superior officer.'

Although the boys were theoretically free to return home on Sundays, considerable pressure was put on them to stay, and their parents to let them do so. Pastor Kahn, the official chaplain to the *Hitler Jugend*, protested in a long indignant memorandum to the

Reichsjugendführer that solely warlike and un-Christian behaviour was being inculcated in the youth on the Sabbath. Von Schirach ignored these protests.

Time was playing into his hands: as the 1930s advanced, the physical training and open air-life superseded any other activity for German youth. The process had only one end – to construct suitable human material as trained fighters for the armed services. This view was echoed obediently by the newspaper *Angriff* (Attack) which wrote that the Hitler Youth represented a new type, a heroic type, the child and youth who

Left: Dr Ley, head of the *Reich* Organization, greets graduates from *Adolf Hitler Schulen* who have distinguished themselves in the front line. Younger members can be seen in the background.

will die for his ideal as the older soldier does in war.' But too often the reality was somewhat different: the new and heroic types were so exhausted after the mandatory weekend camps that they were slumped asleep at their desks on Monday morning.

The indoctrination continued during the week. Youngsters went home from school at the end of the day with instructions to badger their parents for toys that were realistic models of aircraft and tanks. Any parent unwise enough to refuse was apt to find that news of his defiance reached the teacher at the *Adolf Hitler Schulen,* who commonly worked under the sinister shadow of the Gestapo. Arrest could be on the simple charge of being 'unworthy of the name of a German parent.'

NAPOLAS

Attendance at the *Adolf Hitler Schulen* was, however, merely a prelude. Ahead of the younger pupils lay the much more prestigious *Nationalpolitische Erziehungs-anstalten,* the National Political Institutes, or *Napolas.* It was significant that the antecedents of the *Napolas* were the cadet institutes for the training of future officers in Imperial Germany and, more particularly, in Prussia, where they had been founded by King Frederick William I, the father of Frederick the Great. Within these schools, the structure mirrored that of the army. There were 'platoons' rather than school forms, and as far as possible the traditions of an historically famous German regiment were followed. There was considerable emphasis on military exercises, which could include the capture of a defended enemy bridge or being dropped from the sidecar unit in unfamiliar territory.

There was one stumbling block. The law prohibited the handling of firearms by youths under the age of 18 unless supervised by competent adults. Since most marksmanship supervisors were themselves often of the same age, adjudication was required at the highest level. Heinrich Himmler, as national police chief, stepped in, reinterpreting 'competent adult' to include these supervisors. Himmler's influence extended still further. In 1936, he began supplying the Hitler Youth with trainers and weapon instructors from the SS.

NIGHT OF THE LONG KNIVES

The growing power of the SS – and the attendant decline of the SA – was illustrated dramatically during the violent last weekend of June 1934. Hitler, using the pretext of an alleged plot by the Storm Troopers, struck down Ernst Röhm and scores of his followers. The significance of this was not lost on von Schirach, who realized how uncertain the holding of power could be in Nazi Germany. The encroaching militarism of the Hitler Youth was of dubious benefit to him personally, since it served to highlight his own inexperience in service matters. This shortcoming had already been pinpointed by August Heissmeyer, a civil servant specializing in education, who had risen to be a senior inspector within the *Napola*.

Anxious to enhance his own standing, Heissmeyer was careful to curry favour with Bernhard Rust, who in April 1934 had become Education Minister for the Reich. Rust also held the SS rank of *Obergruppenführer*, giving him close access to *SS-Reichsführer* Heinrich Himmler. Furthermore, he was firmly of the opinion that von Schirach lacked the necessary experience and maturity to train an elite. All of which prompted the obvious question: Who did?

Much though Himmler might have wished it, such training could not be carried out effectively by the *SS-Verfügungstruppen* (Combat Troops), the forerunner of the *Waffen-SS* – Armed SS – which was itself in the process of development. Only the Army had the necessary experience and resources, a truth that brought von Schirach into direct conflict with one of its rising members, *Oberstleutnant* Erwin Johannes Eugen Rommel.

Right: *Hitler Jugend* at Wrezen station wait to embark on trains for Brandenburg to help with the harvest in 1939. *Hitler Jugend* members played an increasingly important role in the economy, both before and during the war.

Rommel was the son of a Swabian schoolmaster and held the *Pour le Merité,* Germany's highest decoration of World War I. In 1937, he was an instructor at the War Academy at Potsdam, and he was assigned to the Hitler Youth with the specific task of supervising general standards of training and discipline.

Rommel's relations with von Schirach were strained from the start. The latter's arrogance and self-indulgence, which included a chauffeur-driven car, grated on the older battle-hardened soldier, whose lifestyle was one of almost monkish austerity. In the course of a nationwide tour of the Hitler Youth camps, Rommel made it clear that, though he regarded their personnel as future manpower for the *Wehrmacht,* he felt that they were being overfed on ideology, frequently at the expense of both their basic education and essential paramilitary training. To remedy the situation, Rommel sought to act as mediator between the military and von Schirach. The latter, sensing intrigue, protested vehemently and relations between the two men worsened even further.

Von Schirach's talent for intrigue was unabated. Indeed, Alfred Jodl, Chief of Operations Staff at *Oberkommando der Wehrmacht* (OKW), confided to his diary that the former was 'Trying to break up the close cooperation initiated between the *Wehrmacht* and the *Hitler Jugend* and *Oberstleutnant* Rommel.' Rommel told von Schirach bluntly that, if he wished to be leader of a paramilitary force, he should first become a soldier himself. The dispute led to Rommel's withdrawal, at any rate for the time being, and the cessation of any formal relationship between

Below: Field exercises took on an increasingly aggressive air, which was obviously to the taste of these boys. A wide variety of flags and pennants were used, ranging from crossed swords to skull and crossbones.

Right: Erwin Rommel's bid to assist in the training of a future armed *Hitler Jugend* resulted in a personality clash with Baldur von Schirach which robbed the latter of a valuable source of practical military experience.

the Army and the Hitler Youth. Von Schirach had to content himself with a single act of petty spite: he saw to it that Rommel did not receive the golden badge of the *Hitler Jugend.*

But with Germany intent on war, the SS now took centre stage at the expense of the *Wehrmacht.* It was a logical progression from the 1920s, when the SS formed the nucleus of a fully armed unit, initially as a bodyguard for the Führer but developing to two divisions by 1939. Its influence was profound on one of the Hitler Youth's most elite organisations, the *HJ-Streifendienst,* or Patrol Service. Formed in December 1936, this had acted as an internal police force, keeping order at the rallies and camps. Less than two years later, it was totally reorganized as a sort of preparatory school for the SS. In that year, too, the Hitler Youth was first running weekend courses in field exercises (*Gelandesport*) and rifle shooting. Initially, its own personnel, together with an intake from the *Wehrmacht,* were providing the instructors. Three years later, conditions were very different: weekend courses gave way to toughening-up camps – *Wehrertuchtigungslager* (*WE Lager*). Boys between the ages of $16^{1}/_{2}$ and 18 were put through a three-week course for an award whose purpose was clear – *K-Schein,* or War Training Certificate.

Soon, training was literally taken to the streets. In June 1939, *SS-Gruppenführer* Dr Johannes Meyer, head of the *Feuerschutzpolizei* (Fire Protection Police), met Hitler Youth leaders to set up the *HJ-Feuerloschdienst* (HJ Fire Defence Squads), ready to tackle the effect of air raids on German towns and cities. Even more crucially, in the year that war broke out, the Nazi Party took control of the life of every German boy and girl between the ages of 10 and 18: Hitler Youth membership became compulsory, and ahead lay a war in which the growing shortage of homeland personnel would mean a special task for each child. Singsongs around the campfire all too soon became a distant memory.

Right: *Hitler Jugend* **in 1938 at the last of the Nuremberg rallies. For Nuremberg itself, a citadel of Nazism, it was also a last hurrah. Six years later the Old City became the target for Allied bomber raids.**

CHAPTER TWO

TRAINING

As the war turned against Germany, the Hitler Youth training camps were combed for manpower and ruthless methods of coercion applied. Boys as young as 17 were press-ganged by *Waffen-SS* recruiting officers for a new fighting unit, 12th SS Panzer Division *Hitlerjugend*.

With the outbreak of war in September 1939, the indoctrination of the Hitler Youth was stepped up. In florid terms, the legend of Langemarck continued to be evoked by Nazi propagandists:

'The myth of the sacrifice in the World War of Germany's youth has given to the post-war youth a new faith and a new strength to unfold the ideals of National Socialism... From the experience of the World War was born the idea of National Socialism. Out of its armies came the front line soldier.'

The September 1940 issue of the magazine *Pimpf* treated its readers to a prose poem on 'the gentle heart of the Führer', intoning:

'Now all German hearts belong to the Führer. His hand is the fate of our Fatherland. All that happens, that determines our present, is his will... The hand of the Führer leads us.'

The recruiting offices were besieged by impatient youths prepared to go to almost any lengths to be accepted. HW Koch, himself the member of a unit that was to fight in Berlin in the closing weeks of the war, wrote in his history, *The Hitler Youth*:

Left: This powerful recruitment poster was intended to instil a sense of pride into *Hitler Jugend* members who were encouraged to show their patriotism and sense of duty by joining the *Waffen-SS*.

'Throughout the war, incidents occurred of boys appearing at their local Hitler Youth headquarters complaining that they had been overlooked in their call-up... backing up their claims with their birth certificates. With a shrug of the shoulder and a derogatory remark about some bureaucracy which had yet again failed to do its work properly, they were immediately enrolled in the *Jungvolk*. That the birth certificates had been faked was in most cases only discovered afterwards or when the erasure of the last digit of the year of birth had been carried out too clumsily. Mostly in these cases father or brother had been called up into the army and now the sons too "wanted to do their bit". They were usually allowed to stay.'

NEW LEADER

By this time, Baldur von Schirach had lost all credibility. When he finally succumbed to Rommel's suggestion that he should undertake military training, it was too late to win over both leading Nazis and senior members of the *Wehrmacht*. All had distrusted him from the start. In any case, his training had involved blatantly preferential treatment – not least, a rapid promotion to the rank of *Leutnant* in just six months. His military career was over on 2 August 1940, when he was appointed *Reichsstatthalter* (Governor and Gauleiter) of Vienna. His replacement was his one-time

assistant, 27-year-old Artur Axmann, a man of altogether different stamp. A ruthless organizer, he had at the same time the knack of gaining the respect of subordinates.

Inheritance of 8870 young people between the ages of 10 and 18 did bring problems. More than a quarter of the youth leaders had been called up for the *Wehrmacht*, a shortage which led 16 and 17 year olds to be promoted to the rank of *Unterbannführer*, with responsibility for anything between 500 and 600 boys. The hitherto strict division between *Jungvolk* and Hitler Youth was eventually eliminated, to counter the danger that the young who remained behind while others were experiencing the conflict would become demoralized. Consequently, paramilitary training of Hitler Youth was intensified, often supervised by former members who had been decorated for valour during their service in the *Wehrmacht*.

THE NSKK

Particular efforts were made to appeal to a recruit's special interest. Opportunities were provided for enrolment in the key branches of the forces. In the Army, service was encouraged in the *National-sozialistches Kraftfahr Korps* (NSKK), the motorized branch of *Motor-HJ*, a special formation within the Hitler Youth. Members were required at the age of 16 to attend the *Reichsmotorschule*, to obtain a motorcycle licence. At the age of 18, transfer to the NSKK was possible. Here, thorough grounding was given, not simply in driving, but in mechanics and the international traffic code. Requirements were stringent; members of *Motor-HJ* were required to have 80 hours' driving experience and to have carried out 105 hours of service as a mechanic. No secret was made of the ultimate intention: to produce a ready made cadre for the front line motorized units of the *Wehrmacht*.

For those attracted to service in the air, there was the *National Socialist Flieger Korps* (NSFK), which

Left: HJ volunteers were encouraged to enrol in the key branches of the forces. Here recruits to the *Nationalsozialistches Kraftfahr Korps* (NSKK) are being put through their paces in an early PzKpfw IV tank.

undertook the flying training of the Hitler Youth. This was practical so long as Germany continued on the path of conquest, but from mid-1942, the reconstituted *Flieger-HJ* found itself fulfilling a very different function. The heartlands of the Reich were enduring an ever-accelerating bomber offensive, and the call on the ground now was not for fledgling pilots, but for anti-aircraft personnel. Manpower was plundered from the Hitler Youth as a whole, but, above all, from the *Flieger-HJ*. Senior members manned the guns, while younger ones were mustered to work for the communications network of the flak batteries, at searchlight batteries and as dispatch riders. Schoolchildren became accustomed to *Wehrmacht* soldiers, complete with clipboards and instructions, invading their classrooms. The pupils were required to return home, put on their Hitler Youth uniforms and report for duty as requested by the soldiers.

LEADERSHIP ISSUES

Propaganda minister Josef Göbbels recorded in his diary on 17 December 1942 that Axmann was expressing unease at this role for Hitler Youth:

'He is very much worried lest the draft in of juveniles for anti-aircraft duty might deprive his Hitler Youth leadership corps of its most promising members. About 40,000 well-trained young people are affected. While the anti-aircraft can ill afford to do without them, I believe, nonetheless, that the work of the Hitler Youth must be kept up in all circumstances, especially during the war. The young must be guided by a firm hand as far as possible. If left to themselves, the mischief will be all the greater.'

Germany's change of fortune on the Russian front in no way lessened another of the key activities of the Hitler Youth – international cooperation. As early as 1937, Baldur von Schirach visited Fascist Italy to make contact and arrange exchange visits with youth groups there. Five years later, it was the

Right: The *Motor-HJ* was already thriving when Hitler came to power in 1933. By 1938 28,000 driving licences had been issued to members, many of whom went on to serve in the motorized units of the *Wehrmacht*.

turn of Austria. Artur Axmann joined von Schirach, who also held the sinecure post of Reichsleader for Education of the NSDAP (Nazi Party) in Vienna, where the European Youth League was founded. The so-called 'Culture Day of European Youth' embraced representatives from a wide spread of countries, including the Spanish *Falange*, the Dutch National Socialist Youth and the Norwegian *Nasjional-Samling-Youth*.

MIXED RESPONSE

Within Germany itself, the reaction to the Vienna initiative was mixed. The concept of Germany as a partner in some sort of European alliance was anathema to Göbbels, who ordered a press boycott of the event. His stance was that Germany was fighting a war,

which it would win as the master race; talks of alliances could wait until final victory, but until then the glory would not be shared.

The promotion of good fellowship, however, was by no means the overriding purpose of the German young. Duties in the vassal states had their sinister side. Within days of its occupation, Strasbourg was penetrated by a group of Hitler Youth, extending clandestine activities that dated from the early 1930s. Elsewhere, the Hitler Youth was involved in 'resettlement programmes', such as the expulsion of the native Polish populations from the Warthegau. This was the region of Poland annexed by Germany, where the policy was replacement by native Germans.

However, the 'Culture Day of European Youth' was observed with particular interest by the Swabian

Left: The regional organization of the Hitler Youth in 1942 at the peak of Germany's fortunes in the war. Note the incorporation of Bohemia and Moravia as well as large parts of Poland into the Greater German Reich.

Above: War games had always played a part in the Hitler Youth's programmes from the beginning. Here children in April 1933 practise crawling through undergrowth as if attacking an enemy position.

SS-Brigadeführer Gottlob Berger. As Head of SS Headquarters, he shared with his chief, Heinrich Himmler, a vision of a united Europe within which the *Waffen-SS* would become the central institution of Nazism. All this was in line with Berger's particular responsibility – the raising of pan-European *Waffen-SS* units. He had proved his organizational ability as far back as 1938, when directing the activities of the Czech nationalist Konrad Henlein, founder of the Sudeten German Party, whose structure and ideology were based on the Nazi Party. Within three months

after the outbreak of war, Berger, acting under the instructions of Himmler, had created the *Waffen-SS* Recruiting Office within the SS Main Office (*Hauptamt*), putting himself in control. Recruiting stations were established, and from early 1940, recruitment moved steadily ahead.

Where recruiting was not voluntary, persuasion was adopted. Supported by Dr Robert Ley, the Chief of the German Labour Front (DAF) – the replacement for the former Trade Union movement – the SS drew up a scheme that allowed youths between

Above: Shooting competitions were held frequently at National Training Camps which were set up in 1939. In this picture rifle practice is being undertaken for the benefit of a visiting Nazi dignitary.

Right: Hitler Youth members were increasingly called upon to defend Germany's cities from Allied bombers. They became familiar with anti-aircraft weapons like this quadruple 20mm (0.79in) Flak gun.

the ages of 18 and 20 to be released from customary labour service. There was a proviso, of course: that they volunteered for long-term enlistment in the field units of the SS or within the *Totenkopf* and *Polizei* SS formations.

The task of recruitment was entrusted to *SS-Obergruppenführer* Hans Juttner. He was not above using press gang methods when necessary and endured the indignant reaction of parents who considered their sons to have been railroaded into the SS. In a letter to his father, one Labour Service youth protested:

'Dear Papa,

Today I witnessed the dirtiest trick I have ever seen. Three SS men and a policeman appeared at the camp, demanding that all the inmates register on the *Waffen-SS* recruiting roster… About 60 men were forced to sign, failing which they were given a reprimand or three days under arrest. All sorts of threats were used. Everybody was frightfully indignant. One or two just departed, even through the window. The policeman stood at the door and would let no one out. The whole camp is furious. I've had enough. I've changed completely.'

In the face of such indignation, the SS authorities were obliged to backtrack. A compromise was agreed whereby the youths were to be kept in training for a month or so, then offered the choice of volunteering or quitting the SS service altogether. Berger saw this as a threat to his authority, but was obliged to agree to the measure. At the same time, he stepped up recruitment inducements. In 1939, new National Training Camps (*Wehrertuchtigungslager der HJ*) were established. These were under the command of *HJ Gebeitsführer* (later *SS-Hauptsturmführer*) Gerhard Hein, holder of the Knight's Cross with Oak Leaves.

From a propaganda perspective, Hein was the ideal man for the job. A highly decorated veteran of both the *Wehrmacht* and the *Waffen-SS*, he came from a mining family in Upper Silesia, had joined the Hitler Youth in 1939, and became a camp director in rural Schleswig-Holstein. Under Hein's tutelage,

these youths found instruction even more strenuous than had previously been the case. A War Training Certificate could be earned at the end of three weeks, into which were crammed a range of courses, including field exercises and field shooting. The most important difference between these camps and their predecessors was the increasing role undertaken in them by the *Waffen-SS*, the intention being to marginalize the Army.

ARMY CONFLICT

This, however, was not without its problems for Berger. A recruit who expressed a wish to join the *Waffen-SS* at the end of training could do so only with the blessing of the *Wehrmacht*, which exercised ultimate control. Berger set about looking for ways to exploit the accepted mechanics of recruitment. The solution adopted was for a *Waffen-SS* aspirant, once he had obtained his War Training Certificate at 18, to

apply for the SS well in advance of his date for military conscript service – at age 21. In most cases, his wishes were invariably respected.

The camps were a treasure house for the *Waffen-SS*. By late 1942, that was just as well for Germany. Field Marshal Friederich von Paulus, commander of Sixth Army, who had pressed ahead with his attack on Stalingrad, would ultimately be defeated in early 1943

and obliged to surrender what remained of his army. Overall, 91,000 German soldiers and 24 generals passed into Soviet captivity, leaving behind 70,000 German dead from an army that had once numbered half a million men in total.

The need for fresh recruits was therefore chronic. Yet even before Stalingrad, Axmann, anxious to cement relationships with Berger and Himmler,

Left: *Hitler Jugend* recruits for the *Waffen-SS* are put through their paces for the cameras. Such punishing exercise would have been familiar to the HJ members after their War Training Certificate course.

Above: Once training of the division started in earnest, recruits were still expected to maintain high levels of fitness. This recruit is struggling through mud on a river bank, a good test of his stamina.

secured an interview with the *Reichsführer-SS*. Himmler, against all his previous racial convictions, was increasingly obliged to pin his faith on recruits from the occupied countries of Europe and the East. Axmann pointed out that dedication to the German cause from these sources might be firm, but fighting capability could by no means be taken for granted. However, manpower that came from the National Training Camps, strengthened by solid training at the hands of those who had actually experienced battle conditions, would be another matter. Axmann therefore proposed raising an entire division composed of Hitler Youth volunteers. Himmler's reaction was cautious, but he agreed to raise the matter with Hitler.

German Victory

The defeat at Stalingrad was followed in March 1943 by the German recapture of Kharkov, in the eastern Ukraine, the third time the city had fallen in 18 months. In the process of regaining Kharkov, the Donetz basin with all its rich minerals had been secured. This was a remarkable achievement for the three divisions of II SS Panzer Corps – *Leibstandarte*

Adolf Hitler, Das Reich and *Totenkopf* – which had spearheaded the operation, but at the cost of the lives of 365 officers and 11,154 men. Such losses made a fresh source of manpower an imperative. Hitler, who had at first been reluctant to expand the *Waffen-SS*, preferring to keep it as a small elite, consented eventually to the raising of a new division. The division's strength was to be drawn from those undergoing instruction at training camps throughout the Reich.

DIVISION TITLE

Axmann was told that the division was to carry the title *Hitlerjugend*. It was also suggested that one of the regiment should be named *Herbert Norkus*, after one the Hitler Youth's earliest adherents who had been stabbed to death by Communist opponents in January 1932, but this proposal was ultimately abandoned. Besides, the need for a fresh intake of recruits was decidedly more relevant. Some indication of how

Above: A former member of the Hitler Youth (left), now in the *Leibstantarte*, has his belongings inspected by Adolf Hitler and Sepp Dietrich in 1935. Interchange of personnel between the two organizations was quite usual.

desperate the manpower situation was could be judged by the fact that volunteers were soon being drawn from 17 year olds born between January and June 1926. The normal requirement of a spell in the Labour Service was to be waived.

Once again, reservations expressed by Göbbels threatened to be a stumbling block. The propaganda minister posed an obvious question: 'Would this not suggest to our enemies that Germany had been reduced to calling up children through her weakness?' Even so, on 24 June 1943, 12th SS Panzer Division *Hitlerjugend* was activated.

Recruitment methods became increasingly ruthless. Youths who had volunteered for the *Luftwaffe* or the U-boat section of the Navy, and who had been assured that they were accepted, were all but frog-marched to *Waffen-SS* barracks. There were even instances of sleeping quarters being invaded at night by recruiting officers touting pen and paper.

Within the camps themselves, there was discrimination against those who had chosen to enlist in the *Wehrmacht*. One recruit, Klaus Granzow, outlined his experiences and those of a colleague during training in his diary on 25 July 1943:

Below: Over 200 *Hitler Jugend* and girls listen to an address given by *Reichsjugendführer* Artur Axmann in Dusseldorf in November 1942 after receiving awards for their part in defending Germany from air attack.

'Few in our group volunteered for the SS. The SS sergeant appears every day in our rooms… Klaus Odefey and I then immediately leave the room, since we have both signed up to become officer candidates in the army. They cannot force us into the SS. The others in our group have until tomorrow to think it over. Then they will probably be forced to sign up. In other groups most of the boys signed up with the *Waffen-SS* for 12 years. They can choose their own type of service. Most of them choose tank units. They will now push a light load and have an easy time. Only we officer cadets will be further pushed around. That is absolutely wrong. Why are those of us who are going into the army treated worse than the boys who

are pulled into the SS? Are we not fighting for Germany, the same Fatherland?'

During training, there were the inevitable mishaps and fatalities. Surviving *Waffen-SS* documents reveal details of many fatal accidents involving firearms, mostly pistols. There were also regular monthly reports on desertion (*Fahnenflucht*) and suicide or attempted suicide. Seven pages of a single document explained how to deal with the corpses of those who died in training or on active service. It was accompanied by an illustration of an approved wooden cross for a grave for all ranks. No such grave was allowed, however, for 'dishonourable suicides and those shot under martial law'. Neither could such deaths be granted burial in a military cemetery. A standard letter to be sent to the parents of those who died in action urged them to see '…your son's heroic death as a step on the way to the victory of the Greater German State and our philosophy of life [*Weltanschauung*]'. Before being despatched to the dead youth's family, however, the communication had to gain the approval of the appropriate *Ortsgruppenleiter* (Political Leader).

INEXPERIENCE

Burgeoning recruiting figures did not, of course, solve the problem of inexperience. The division was therefore obliged to turn to the elite of the SS formations, the *Leibstandarte Adolf Hitler,* which had been the first *Waffen-SS* unit to be formed and whose origins dated from the early days of the Nazi movement, when it had formed the Führer's personal bodyguard. Creamed off from the disgruntled *Leibstandarte,* which regarded itself as a stand-alone elite, were all the regimental, battalion and company commanders, together with an entire *Panzerjägerabteilung* (anti-tank battalion), a complete medical clearing station from the Medical Battalion, and 11 senior NCOs and 120 men. The first commander of the new division, Fritz

Right: Artur Axmann visits members of the new *Hitlerjugend* Division. He is using his left hand because his right arm below the elbow was severed while he was serving on the Russian front earlier in the war.

Witt, had previously commanded the 1st SS Panzer Grenadier Regiment of the *Leibstandarte,* where he had distinguished himself in Poland and Russia. In July 1943, he was promoted to *SS-Brigadeführer und Generalmajor der Waffen-SS,* thus making him at the age of 35 the second youngest general in Germany's armed forces. But alongside talent of this calibre had to be set men of infinitely less experience, who became company commanders when they had experience only of commanding a platoon.

Berger and his cohorts had initially assumed a manpower of 830 officers and 4000 NCOs. The losses experienced by the *Leibstandarte* while fighting on the

Below: A panzergrenadier in Normandy in June 1944. Although German units usually possessed a higher weight of personal firepower than their Allied equivalents, Mauser bolt-action rifles were still common weapons.

southern wing in Russia between 1942 and 1943 had been crippling, particularly during the abandonment and subsequent recapture of Kharkov. A further drain was caused by the outcome of Operation Citadel, the ultimately abortive German attempt in July 1943 to cut out the Russian salient around Kursk.

Waffen-SS combatants who had distinguished themselves on the Russian front were sent on conducted tours of recruitment centres, and presented as role models to volunteers. *SS-Unterscharführer* Fritz Kristen, a gunner in the *SS-Totenkopf* Division, had been the first man to receive the Knight's Cross, with which he had been decorated by the Führer himself. The sole survivor of his battery, he had held off Soviet tank assaults while under constant fire. Isolated from his unit, and without food and water, he blazed away at Soviet tanks and infantry. After 72 hours, his toll was 13 tanks and around 100 Russian dead. The feat, as

Above: Most of the division's tanks were not the latest Panthers, but up-gunned and up-armoured PzKpfw IVs. This *Hitlerjugend* example has been covered in foliage to camouflage it from Allied aircraft.

presented to impressionable young recruits, made Kristen an instant role model. Mustered to tour the recruiting stations, he told colourful versions of his exploits, shadowed by the full resources of Göbbels' propaganda apparatus.

RISING PROBLEMS

Behind the scenes and away from the rhetoric, problems grew. Not the least of these was the provision of uniforms and armour. As late as November, the division was able to muster only 10 tanks, and until the end of the war remained short of its authorized establishment. At the start of the division's life, one of its panzer regiments that was formed near Reims could boast just four serviceable PzKpfw IVs and Panther

tanks. These particular tanks had literally been stolen from the Eastern Front, in direct defiance of *Wehrmacht* orders. Others had been 'requisitioned' from the virtually defunct Italian Army. These turned out to be a dangerous liability, since breakdowns were common and repairs frequently could not be carried out because of lack of spares. On the other hand, field and anti-tank guns were reported to be in healthy supply, but transport trucks numbered 2214, just half the paper allocation.

In July and August 1943, the initial band of recruits, some 100,000 strong, arrived in Beverloo, Belgium, for further training. Many were barely 17 years old. Others were mustered in the provinces of Antwerp and Limburg, and the French military training area of Mailly-le-Camp. Training was geared to likely impending operations and was almost entirely devoted to firearms for use in field combat. The 12th SS Panzer Division *Hitlerjugend* was in the process of being blooded for war.

CHAPTER THREE

ORGANIZATION

Iron discipline within the ranks of the service echelons of the Hitler Youth extended to the correct wearing of uniform and insignia according to rank. The shortages due to the war, however, meant that the *Hitlerjugend* Division had anything but a uniform appearance.

During the early days of the 12th SS Panzer Division *Hitlerjugend*, it was virtually impossible for hard and fast rules to be laid down on uniform and insignia. In many cases, there were insufficient uniforms available to meet demand, and training was often done in standard Hitler Youth uniform. Indeed, so chronic was the situation at one point that uniforms were adopted which were made from surplus Italian camouflage material. A surviving photograph of 'Panzer' Meyer shows him wearing a field cap and blouse made from the Italian material. Italian motor transport and other materials were used to replace German losses, and items of German U-boat clothing, supplied originally to Italy by Germany, were requisitioned after Italy's armistice with the Allies and issued to *Hitlerjugend* tank crews in Normandy.

In many cases, often through sheer necessity, due to the shortage of materials, normal service dress was worn by many. Some of the foreign *Waffen-SS* volunteers in the *Wiking* Division tended to stick to the uniform of their particular Fascist youth organization. Members from the *Leibstandarte* (*LAH*) who joined

Left: These two members of the *Hitlerjugend* division wearing regulation *Waffen-SS* camouflage smocks are seen with a 7.92mm (0.31in) MG 42 machine gun. The gun fired so rapidly that it sounded like tearing linen.

the new *Hitlerjugend* unit continued to wear their existing uniforms with the *LAH* cuff title, also retaining the *LAH* monogram on their shoulder straps.

On the right side of the collar patch, SS-runes were worn, while rank patches appeared on the left side. In the closing phases of the war, Himmler issued an order that the wearing of collar patches on the greatcoat was to cease because of the shortage of raw materials. The rank of *Reichsjugendführer* was the only Hitler Youth rank making use of collar patches. (Incidentally, some idea of the high regard with which Himmler regarded Artur Axmann can be gathered from the fact that the *Reichsjugendführer* bore collar patches very similar to those of the *Reichsführer-SS*.) As for shoulder straps, the basic colour for the strap was black for all Hitler Youth personnel, regardless of rank.

STRONG LINKS

Links with the *Leibstandarte* remained strong. Indeed, the *Hitlerjugend* Division was to incorporate the *LAH* Division's symbol into their own design, particularly as insignia on vehicles. This was a key set into a *Sig*, or victory rune. The choice of a 'key' was significant – the German word for a skeleton key is 'Dietrich', the name of the *LAH*'s founder, Sepp Dietrich.

Camp trainees had military style field-grey tunics bearing no insignia. Another working dress was a

'rush-green' uniform. Headgear was a forage cap with the *Hitler Jugend* diamond badge on the front. The HJ brassard on the front was often the sole one worn.

Regulations on dress and bearing were rigid. In his book *The Hitler Youth,* David Littlejohn gives a detailed account of uniforms and insignia, revealing that to obtain a uniform in the first place, recruits had to surrender wartime coupons and make purchases at *Braune Laden* (brown shops), which supplied appropriate clothing and insignia.

The regular wartime winter service dress consisted of a black ski cap and a dark blue HJ winter blouse with matt silver buttons and patch breast pockets with centre pleats and buttoned flaps. For the summer, there was a brown blouse with wide collar, light brown convex buttons, and patch breast pockets with centre pleats and buttoned flaps.

With this dress, as with all others, clear differences of style existed between ranks, and any infringements were dealt with severely. Winter greatcoats were midbrown with black lapel facings, and senior officers were entitled to gold piping around the collar and cap, together with a gold chin strap. Junior officers had a silver chin strap. Caps worn with winter service dress by Warrant Officer grades – *Gefolgschaftsführer* to *Hautgefolgschaftsführer* – did not carry black bands.

DRACONIAN MEASURES

Within months of his appointment as commander of the division, Fritz Witt issued an order to all his senior officers that, if necessary, they were to take 'draconian measures' against lax bearing and perfunctory saluting by the other ranks. Furthermore, all privately owned weaponry was to be either sent home or surrendered. No man was permitted to leave camp without his bayonet. There was also a sharp reminder from Witt that schooldays belonged to the past, and sports badges were forbidden: 'A soldier wears his war

Left: Many of the *Hitlerjugend*'s NCOs and officers came from the *Leibstandarte Adolf Hitler* Division, forming a tough backbone. This photograph shows a *Leibstandarte* halftrack with the divisional insignia, a skeleton key.

decorations.' Peaked caps were the sole province of higher ranks and drivers only. Of the junior ranks, *Sturmmann* (equivalent to Corporal) displayed the cuff title *Hitlerjugend*, which was awarded to the division as a whole in recognition of its showing in Normandy in September 1944. The style was in imitation of Hitler's handwriting, in white or silver block letters on a black band with silver edging. *Sturmmann*

were supplied with distinctive camouflage smocks and steel helmets.

Among the most senior members, a certain latitude over uniform wear was permitted. Thus a 1944 photograph of von Schirach, taken near Vienna, shows him wearing the basic uniform of the Hitler Youth with the insignia of a National Socialist *Reichleiter*. Von Schirach was also proud to sport a

Left: A machine gun team in the garden of a chateau near Caen in Normandy in 1944. The machine gun team was a key element in German infantry tactics, providing enough firepower to pin down the enemy.

Above: *Hitlerjugend* **Division Panthers parked in a French village soon after D-Day. They are covered with foliage in an attempt to disguise themselves from the Allied reconnaissance and fighter-bomber aircraft.**

Grossdeutschland cuff title, since this was the elite *Wehrmacht* division with which he had performed his short-lived military service. On the other hand, until the closing months of the war, Artur Axmann was tireless in his bid to boost the morale of his men. In September 1944, for example, he was pictured at Kaiserlautern in Germany distributing *Hitlerjugend* cuff titles to new recruits.

CEREMONIALS

One reason why the Hitler Youth was able to assume the mantle of a *Waffen-SS* division comparatively

smoothly is that the movement always had a military ethos. The core unit of the Hitler Youth movement was the *Bann* – roughly equivalent to a military regiment. There were about 300 *Bann* to be found throughout the Reich, each commanding a strength of at least 6000 and each keen to express its own identity. This was manifest in a strong addiction to flags and pennants, borne out by the anthem *Vorwärts, Vorwärts,* written by Baldur von Schirach, with its closing line, '*Ja, die Fahne ist mehr als der Tod*' (Yes, the flag is more to us than death). Each unit carried the same flag, a black swastika against the colours red and

white, 200 x 145 cm (80 x 58 in). At the same time, each unit displayed its individual *Bann* number in black on the yellow scroll above the head of the eagle. The design on both sides was identical, the eagle facing to the staff on the left side and to the fly on the right side. A further emphasis on the military was the display of a black eagle, a design owing its origins to the former Imperial State of Prussia. A tribute to the nationalism of National Socialism was symbolized by a black sword, while a black hammer represented socialism. There were separate flags displayed by *HJ Gefolgschaft* – equivalent to a company of some 150

youths – who proudly displayed panels identifying their individual branches.

New flags ascribed to units of 12th SS Panzer Division *Hitlerjugend* received elaborate dedication ceremonies. In a photograph of one such ceremony, Artur Axmann is seen holding a corner of an existing standard, pressing it against the new flag – a gesture signifying the passing of the old to the new. This incidentally was a deliberate copy of the manner in which Hitler dedicated party standards, on those occasions using the sacred *Blutfahne* (blood banner), marked with the blood of an early Nazi

Left: Young boys of the Hitler Youth march on parade with their banners aloft. Each section attached great pride to their flags, and this devotion to a flag as symbol of the unit was transferred to the *Hitlerjugend* Division.

Below: These young-looking members of the division serving in Normandy are proud recipients of the Iron Cross, thanks to their bravery in combat. The Iron Cross had been reintroduced as a combat award by Hitler.

martyr. As Philip Baker points out in his book *Youth Led by Youth,* flags had a major role to play in training. Elaborate 'battles' were staged as war games, the object being for one unit to capture the flag of another. One such game was accompanied by a rousing commentary:

'The Leader marshals his forces… Our Leader has crossed to his bosom the flag, which is in great peril. Leader fights against Leader, surrounded by a knot of boys. Then a cry goes up from our ranks:'

Below: *Hitlerjugend* **pioneers throw sweets to local children in France in July 1944. Some of the division's members were little older than the boys watching at the back of the crowd.**

"The flag is saved." The battle has cost us a hole in somebody's head, a hole in the flag, two camping knives (*Fahrtenmesser*)…'

'But our flag has withstood its baptism of fire.'

The veneration extended to flags went even further. When these were flown in camps, either for an overnight stop or for a longer duration, they received special guards, and the area in which they stood was regarded as sacred ground. The Hitler Youth was one of only six uniformed organizations whose flag and standard bearers wore special machine-woven arm badges on the upper right arm.

Any attempt at a study of Hitler Youth daggers must be cautious, since many unofficial designs were produced in limited editions by private firms to cash

Above: A rare moment of relaxation before the Allied invasion. To be posted to France was rightly considered to be one of the 'softest' postings in the German Army, even though the Allied invasion was sure to come.

in on what was a growing market and these knives had no official sanction from the organization itself. A regular issue was the *Fahrtenmesser* (travelling or camping knife), which continued to be standard issue until the end of the war. Officers sported an elaborate

affair with the motto, '*Mehr sein als scheinen*' (Be more than you seem).

A ceremonial sword for all Hitler Youth leader ranks, ornamented with the *HJ* diamond swastika, was introduced as early as 1937. Its straight blade was etched on the obverse with *Blut und Ehre* (blood and honour). The scabbard was steel within a dark blue leather wrap and silver-plated fittings, and its upper locket was ornamented in relief with the *HJ* eagle clutching the sword and hammer.

Right: Field Marshal Gerd von Rundstedt, Commander-in-Chief West, inspects members of the *Hitlerjugend* Division in the spring of 1944. He carries his Field Marshal's baton in his right hand.

MUSIC

As was the case with many of the units of both the *Wehrmacht* and the SS, particularly the *Leibstandarte,* music and song formed an important part of cere-monial, even if such trappings had to be curtailed in the face of total war. The Hitler Youth was no excep-tion, with its tradition of camp fire concerts. In con-trast to formal occasions, such concerts were encour-aged as morale boosters, and included traditional folk songs accompanied by guitars, accordians and the mouth organ.

Musicians in bands were distinguished by wearing on their uniform dress, wings known as *Schwalben-nester* – swallows' nests. (This was a reference to the shape of the mud nests which swallows build under the eaves of buildings.) The wings of drum and fife bands tended to have no fringe, and braiding of a dull grey. By contrast, trumpeters had bright braid-ing. Indeed, trumpeters tended to be regarded as a race apart; the long fanfare trumpet, with its red and white banner, soon became the symbol of the youth movement. The trumpet was made from nickel-plate or brass, and decorated with a flag trimmed in black and red, and fringed in aluminium or silver.

There were a variety of shallow drums, including the popular *Landsknecht* (the so-called 'Mercenary') deep drum, many of them carrying the unit name. The larger bands could include a bass drum and brass instruments, headed by a *Schellenbaum* ('Jingling Johnny') which consisted of a plentitude of bells. Modelled very much on the *Schellenbaum* of the *Leibstandarte,* this was patterned after a version that had been used by the German Imperial Army. Musical units received their training from bandmasters seconded from the *Wehrmacht* or various party organizations.

From 1934 onwards, the *Reichsjugendführer* coined an annual slogan indicating which aspect of Hitler Youth activity was to be emphasized in the coming 12 months. Viewed in retrospect, each slogan appears to

chart the progress of the movement. Thus the first slogan was 'Year of Training', followed by 'Year of Toughening Up'. Until the war, the choice was often innocuous, such as 'Year of Hostel Building' for 1937 and 'Year of Getting Acquainted' for 1938. With the

onset of war, the tone understandably turned more militant: 'Year of Testing or Year of Trial' for 1940; 'Our Life, a Road to the Führer' for 1941; and 'Service in the East and on the Land' for 1942. By the time of the formation of the *Hitlerjugend* Division, the slogans were, for 1943, 'War Service of the German Youth' and, striking a somewhat desperate note for 1944, 'The Year of the War Volunteers'.

Some exceptional qualities of leadership were to be found among the founder members of the 12th SS

Panzer Division *Hitlerjugend*. The reasons for this could be traced back to 1932, the year before Hitler attained power. Hartmann Lauterbacher, a deputy to Baldur von Schirach, created the Leo Schlageter School, its name a tribute to an early pro-Nazi martyr, shot by the French during the 1923 Rhineland occupation. The following year it was located in Potsdam and became the first *Reichsführerschule*, or Reich Leadership School. Indeed, by the end of 1933, some 23 leadership schools of one kind or another had opened.

Thus members of the new division were in good shape by the time that they reached the training camp at Beverloo. The division was swiftly organized into two infantry regiments, one panzer regiment, one artillery regiment, one engineer battalion, and a detachment each of reconnaisance, anti-tank, anti-aircraft and signalling groups.

In his book *Grenadiere,* Kurt Meyer, the successor to Fritz Witt, traced how this had already been made possible within the Hitler Youth: 'Many old fashioned principles of military training had to be replaced by new ones, which in their final analysis had their origins in the German youth movement.' Among those principles regarded as outmoded was the long-established relationship between officers and men, dating back to Prussian times. This relationship was now considerably relaxed and an informal atmosphere encouraged. From the earliest days, 'square-bashing' and goose-stepping were eschewed, while route marching was considered both harmful and unnecessary. Rather, there was an emphasis on replicating as far as possible the sort of conditions to be encountered on the battlefield. Among the suggestions put forward by General Heinz Guderian, one of

Left: A *Hitlerjugend* halftrack on exercise near the division's headquarters at Beverloo, Belgium, in the spring of 1944. The veterans drafted in from the *Leibstandarte* gave the division much-needed experience.

Above: The *Hitlerjugend* Division moves up to the front in Normandy. A motorcycle sidecar combination leads a convoy of *Kubelwagen*s, the German equivalent of the American jeep.

Germany's leading exponents of armoured warfare, was that rifle practice on shooting ranges with live ammunition should be discontinued in favour of field exercises. Other fundamentals included learning the importance of effective camouflage and how to monitor the enemy's radio signals.

MILITARY TRAINING

From 1942 onwards, all Hitler Youths received 160 hours of pre-military training. This included small bore shooting and fieldcraft. Thus, by the time the *Hitlerjugend* division was in operation, there were sufficient *schiesswarten* (firearms instructors) for young recruits, all of whom received a 'green licence' and a green cuff band. Indeed, all were taught that a

soldier's best friend was his rifle. Thus, use and care of small-calibre weapons and target shooting took up at least a quarter of training time. By the outbreak of war, some 12,000 youths had taken part in training courses with air rifles, while 51,500 had attained a sufficient skill to receive the Shooting Badge. With the formation of 12th SS Panzer Division *Hitlerjugend*, a further 1,500,000 young men were put through shooting courses, which included instruction in the use of small-calibre guns.

During general training, Fritz Witt laid down three priorities: physical fitness, character training and weapon training. In order to earn the Hitler Youth Proficiency Badge, youths were expected to demonstrate expertise in the use of air rifles,

grenade throwing (with dummies), route marching with full kit, and such field exercises as map reading, distance judging, and the effective use of terrain and camouflage; points that could be scored in tests varied with the age of participants.

HEAVY WEAPONS

During the offensive in Normandy in 1944, the SS panzergrenadiers of I SS Panzer Corps (of which the *Hitlerjugend* Division was a part) were issued with various weapons, the best known of which were the MP 38 and MP 40 sub-machine guns and the 7.92mm (0.31in) MG 42. The MP 38 and MP 40, with lightweight folding stocks and long 32-round magazines, proved more than a match for the British Sten. Infantry battalions also had available towed 75mm (2.95in) light guns with a rate of fire of up to 12 rounds a minute and a range of 4500m (14,765ft).

As for armour, the 101st SS Heavy Panzer Battalion of I SS Panzer Corps had at its disposal the 57-ton Tiger tank with its 88mm (3.45in) gun and three 7.92mm (0.31in) machine guns. Much vaunted in Nazi propaganda, the Tiger had first been demonstrated in 1942 – on 20 April, Hitler's birthday. First used in action on the Russian front in September of that year, and almost invulnerable in North Africa during 1943, the Tiger emerged from a design of the Henschel firm. With maximum armour protection of 11cm (4.4in) on the turret and 10cm (4in) on the hull, the Tiger weighed well over 50 tons, but was ultimately under-powered.

Hitlerjugend's tank regiment was equipped with the Panther, regarded widely as the best tank produced by any nation during the war, weighing around 45 tons, and the PzKpfw IV, an older design still capable of holding its own on the battlefield. The Panther, equipped with a high velocity 75mm (2.95in) gun, repeatedly demonstrated its superiority over the British Cromwell and Churchill tanks.

Left: A *Hitlerjugend* SdKfz 251 halftrack moving across a Normandy field south of Caen accompanied by some panzergrenadiers. The two leading soldiers are a machine gun crew: one carries the MG 42 gun, the other its stand.

CHAPTER FOUR

NORMANDY

Following the Allied landings in Normandy, the untested *Hitlerjugend* Division was drawn into the defence of Caen. Obeying Hitler's inflexible policy of no withdrawal, they were subjected to endless air attacks and artillery and naval bombardments.

It was clear by the end of 1943 that the coming year in the West would be decisive for the fortunes of Germany. Near certainty that the Allies would be landing in France, and that all available forces must be concentrated there, led to even more feverish recruitment for the 12th SS Panzer Division *Hitlerjugend*. There were increased incidents of the enforced drafting of teenagers, along with shoals of complaints from parents. The Nazi Party Secretary, Martin Bormann, drew Himmler's attention to the rising discontent, reporting that 'Men were forced to enlist against their will. Pencils were pressed into their hands accompanied by accusations of treason if they refused to sign up.'

Bormann added that signatures had been elicited under false pretences, the youths being told smoothly that their signatures simply confirmed that literature they were given had been read and understood or that its personal accuracy had been confirmed. Such complaints were brushed aside by the *Reichsführer-SS*, who claimed that permission to open recruits by these methods had been approved by Hitler. Many

complaints were turned over to Gottlob Berger, who, resentful at attempts to undermine his authority, backed Himmler by claiming that most of the recruiting officers were veteran Hitler Youth leaders 'with the necessary experience to handle boys'. Besides, everything had to be subordinated to the Führer's intention of having two divisions in place in France. Himmler went on to plead for cooperation from party chiefs rather than 'constant carping criticism'. In the event, no action was taken over the accusations of coercion; recruitment, by whatever method, continued.

DECLINE

The SS, however, was disturbed by the sharp decline in the number of volunteers. Many of those inducted stated that they feared the disapproval of parents and priests. In the Donauwörth district of Swabia, for example, *SS-Unterscharführer* Gustav Tinnacher, a recruiting officer, reported that his attempts to lure local youth into volunteering for the *Waffen-SS* had been frustrated by 'the pronounced anti-SS attitude of a strongly religious population'.

Recruitment was also hampered by a new fear of combat, born largely from reports from the battlefield at Kharkov. There, despite eventual victory, the casualty rate had been high. Previously, recruiters had

Left: A *Hitlerjugend* armoured car amid the rubble of Caen, scene of violent fighting in June and July 1944. The fall of the city on 18 July was a stepping-stone for the Allied forces onto the rolling plains leading towards Paris.

appealed to Nazi ideology and racial Nordic superiority; now, changing fortunes were making such considerations appear increasingly hollow.

At its formation, 12th SS Panzer Division *Hitlerjugend* was trained by a cadre from the *Leibstandarte*. A new panzer corps was created from these two divisions, named I SS Panzer Corps. It came

under the command of Sepp Dietrich, who also supervised the raising of the *Hitlerjugend* Division.

WAITING GAME

By the end of 1943, only one question remained: where would the Allies invade? For months, the Allies had done their best to deceive their enemy into

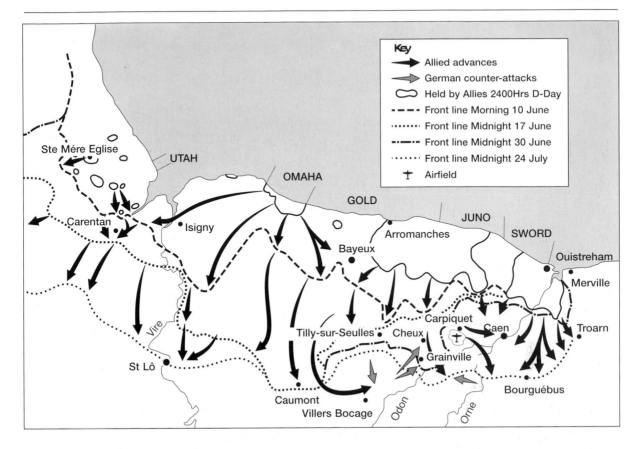

Key
→ Allied advances
⇒ German counter-attacks
⊂⊃ Held by Allies 2400Hrs D-Day
- - - Front line Morning 10 June
······ Front line Midnight 17 June
-·-·- Front line Midnight 30 June
······ Front line Midnight 24 July
✝ Airfield

Ste Mére Eglise
UTAH
OMAHA
GOLD
JUNO
SWORD
Carentan
Isigny
Arromanches
Ouistreham
Merville
Bayeux
Vire
Carpiquet
Tilly-sur-Seulles
Cheux
Caen
Troarn
St Lô
Grainville
Bourguébus
Caumont
Odon
Orne
Villers Bocage

Left: Half-hidden from prying Allied aircraft, a truck of the *Hitlerjugend* Division shortly after D-Day. The division's actions on D-Day helped prevent the Allies reaching one of their prime objectives: Caen.

Above: A map showing the Allied progress inland after D-Day. The *Hitlerjugend* were heavily involved in the defence of Caen, fighting just to the west of the city until its eventual fall.

expecting a major assault against the Pas-de-Calais. On D-Day itself, an elaborate technical deception led German radar operators to report vast air and sea fleets approaching the Calais area.

Early on the morning of 6 June, however, the size of the airborne landings indicated to Field Marshal Gerd von Rundstedt that the invasion was coming along the Normandy coast. He also reasoned that it scarcely mattered if the Normandy assault was indeed a feint – they would surely build on what they achieved. He therefore believed that all available force should be used to counter the attack. However, the two panzer divisions he was keen to move were not under his authority, but were held in reserve by the *Oberkommando der*

Wehrmacht (OKW, or German Army High Command). To save time, he first issued orders for each division to move and only then notified OKW, seeking its approval. This was not forthcoming, and he was informed by *Generaloberst* (Colonel-General) Alfred Jodl that the two divisions would not be committed until orders were received from Hitler. Von Runstedt could only order the flak units of both divisions, which had become separated, to be placed on alert, ready to join their parent formations when required.

All the while, despite discouraging weather, numerous Allied parachute and glider landings were going ahead as well as assaults on five separate beaches. Acres of Normandy earth shuddered as thousands

Above: SS panzergrenadiers move over open ground towards Caen. If the *Hitlerjugend* Division allowed the Allies to reach this open ground, the numerical superiority of the Allied armour would overwhelm them.

Right: The Allied breakout from Normandy squeezed the *Hitlerjugend* and other German units into an ever-decreasing 'pocket' south of Falaise, as Patton and Free French forces approached from the south.

of Allied bombers and fighter bombers released their loads, while the coast became an inferno of explosion and fire from naval guns.

FARCE

German preparations in Normandy – or rather, the lack of them – had their farcical side. The sole mobile reserve that the Germans possessed was 21st Panzer Division, whose commander, Edgar Feuchtinger, could not be located and was later said to have been dallying with a woman in Paris. Field Marshal Rommel, commanding Army Group B and responsible for the coastal defences of northern France, was in Swabia attending his wife's birthday, and had left his chief of staff, Lieutenant General Hans Speidel, in charge. Meanwhile, many senior commanders were engaged in war games at Rennes in Brittany. Sepp Dietrich, commander of I SS Panzer Corps, to which the 12th SS and *Panzer Lehr* Divisions were subordinate, was in Brussels. The weather in the Channel was

so poor the Germans believed that the invasion would not be until the next full moon. The German chain of command thus ran upwards from Speidel to von Rundstedt, who was out of reach in his headquarters outside Paris, and continued up to *Führerhauptquartier* (Führer Headquarters), by that time temporarily installed in the Berghof at Berchtesgarden. Only from there could it course down again, to reach the panzer division commanders. This all required time, and time is expensive in a major emergency.

At first, Speidel was oblivious to the dangers, hosting a dinner party at the very time the first parachutes were landing. With the news breaking, he signalled Rommel to return. It was not until 08:00 that the first Panzer battalion started moving north towards the vital defensive area around Caen.

Vital minutes continued to ticked away. At 10:00, Field Marshal Keitel finally spoke to Hitler, who had been sleeping late as usual. Only then did he ring von Rundstedt's headquarters. Forever his master's voice, he stressed that there could be no question of the Panzer reserves being placed under the latter's command. As a concession, *Hitlerjugend* was allowed to edge up the coast, but it remained firmly under the control of OKW. The *Panzer Lehr* Division was to stay where it was.

For the Allies, Caen was to be the first French town of consequence that the liberation armies were likely to enter. Its value was in its location, above all as the centre of Norman road and rail communications. At its northern neck lay a plain large enough for the construction of an airfield complex. From here, it would be possible to develop major armoured

operations striking out towards Falaise. What is more, its position in the extreme northwest of the zone covered by Army Group B meant that it was the obvious point of concentration for German armour. Thus Caen was writ large in Allied D-Day objectives.

To the northeast of Caen – which was some 16 km (10 miles) inland from the Allied 'Sword' beach – Royal Marine Commandos landed with infantry divisions and Special Service brigades, intending to push south and east out of the beachhead. Von Rundstedt and his operations chief, General Gunther Blumentritt, were frustrated by the delay that let the Allies steadily consolidate their position. They came

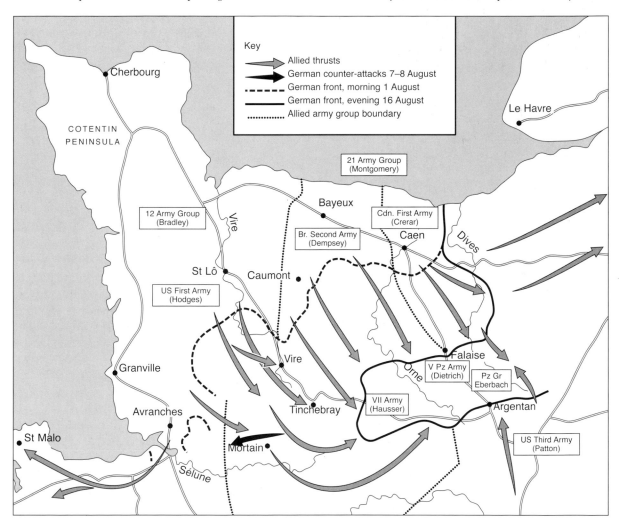

Stuttgarter Jllustrierte

STADT DER AUSLANDSDEUTSCHEN
Nr. 25   21. Juni 1944   20 Pfg.

INVASION!
Die deutschen Gegenmaßnahmen laufen!

Above: During the battle of Normandy, there was no shortage of propaganda extolling the role and daring of the *Hitlerjugend*. On this magazine cover, members of the division are seen waiting for the next Allied attack.

ashore on five beaches – and the possibility of driving them back into the sea was becoming more difficult with each hour that passed. It was not until 14:30 that OKW announced a change of heart. Rundstedt was handed not only the 17th SS and *Panzer Lehr* Divisions, but also Sepp Dietrich's I SS Panzer Corps, which included the *Hitlerjugend* Division.

For Fritz Witt, commander of the *Hitlerjugend,* the journey to the front was a nightmare, taking eight hours, four of which were spent in roadside ditches, dodging air attacks. For good measure, he reported that the division's marching columns had suffered serious losses in men and material. In deployment

west of Paris and south of Rouen, the SS corps was soon on the move for Normandy, the tranquil June air shattered by the roar of Panzer engines and the sharp scream of tank tracks. Riding on their division's Mark IV tanks, panzergrenadiers wore hastily applied camouflage foliage, while motorcycle combinations and scout cars sped past. Ahead of them, to a maximum depth of 25km (40 miles), lay countryside consisting mainly of small fields bounded by stout hedge-topped banks, known as bocage. Woodlands and orchards were fractured by high-banked lanes and muddy-bottomed streams, studded with stout stone villages and farmsteads.

WITTMANN

Among these forces on the morning of 6 June were not only Fritz Witt and 'Panzer' Meyer, but also the formidable *SS-Obersturmführer* Michael Wittmann, who during the battle of Kursk in the previous year had accounted for 30 Soviet tanks, 28 anti-tank guns and two artillery batteries. With the *Hitlerjugend* was *SS-Obersturmbannführer* Max Wünsche, a product of the elite *SS-Junkerschule* Bad Tölz. All were at the disposal of Rommel's Army Group B, and were ordered to the area of Liseux, prior to regrouping west of Caen for the counter-attack against Canadian forces.

They had one serious disadvantage, however: the lack of air cover. RAF Hawker Typhoons took full advantage during daylight hours, firing both low-level rocket and cannon attacks. Heavy shells fired from warships offshore whistled overhead. And this was just the start of problems. The 2nd Battalion of the 12th SS Panzer Regiment was held up: the Panzer tanks of its 1st Battalion were stranded by a lack of fuel on the east bank of the Orne river, and there was little prospect of obtaining any quickly. Rommel was thus unable to deploy the whole division for the counter-attack and was forced to depend on a *Kampfgruppe* (literally 'battle group') under the command of Kurt

Right: The best tanks available to the division in Normandy were Panthers, armed with a high-velocity 75mm (2.95in) gun. Panthers could knock out advancing Allied Churchills and Shermans with virtual impunity.

'Panzer' Meyer. Not long before, Meyer had described the invaders as 'little fish', predicting that they would soon be beaten back into the sea by the pick of the *Hitlerjugend*.

Meyer, a former policeman and the illegitimate son of a labourer, had joined the *Leibstandarte* Adolf Hitler in May 1934. A mere 1.75 metres (5ft 8in) in height, he was obliged to wear a raised orthopedic left shoe because of a serious leg injury. But in three years, he had reached the rank of *SS-Haupsturmführer*,

in command of a motorcycle company. Service in Greece had brought him the Knight's Cross, and he won his Oakleaves in 1943 on the Russian front.

Now his *Kampfgruppe* consisted of one tank battalion with 90 Mark IVs and three infantry battalions plus artillery. These he intended to insert on the left of 21st Panzer Division to drive together to the beach. But Canadian strength was building up, and Meyer decided to attack fast, a decision that came to naught when the enemy mounted a vicious riposte. Meyer

was able to judge something of its effect himself: during a conversation with a battalion commander, a tank shell split their meeting place wide open, decapitating the other man in the process.

The objective of the main German counter-offensive was to split the beachhead. Three tank companies were placed in position. The *Hitlerjugend* could muster two armoured battalions and two panzer-grenadier regiments, with reconnaissance, engineer and artillery contingents. As back-up, Meyer selected

the tall buildings of Ardenne Abbey as his forward command post, its towers affording a commanding view of Caen's western edge. One of his first actions was to move forward badly-needed fuel; he organized a shuttle of jerry cans, which were loaded aboard Volkswagen field cars.

The Allies were struggling in the nearby area of Cambes. The 3rd Infantry Division of the Ulster Rifles had not known the whereabouts of the Germans since the woods and park at Cambes were protected by stone walls more than 1 metre (3¹/₂ ft) high. The Germans took full advantage of their position and poured forth infantry and mortar fire, causing severe casualties and forcing a withdrawal.

ADVANCE

Meanwhile, the 12th SS Panzer Division advanced, and in its forefront was the 1st Platoon of the Heavy Infantry Gun Company. The platoon possessed only short-range guns and had to advance with the lines of infantry, bereft of armour. Some 50 metres (164ft) in front, a Sherman rumbled out of a side road, its turret immediately swinging towards the Germans. The first shell was fired and the men of the platoon were saved by jumping over a locked gate. They sought refuge in a farm, grateful that the shells were anti-tank rather than explosive, which would have put paid to every man. They made contact with a single infantryman who had previously gone missing and who had one *Panzerfaust* anti-tank rocket. This was used to disable a Sherman, blocking the main intersection for the passage of any following tanks.

At Malon, another wooded area north of Cambes, a shell exploded on treetops. The trees then fell on a Panzer, hitting its centre and putting paid to any visibility. To make matters worse, the turret stuck fast. The decision of two other passing tanks to stop and open fire proved fatal: both were hit, one losing a track while the other kept up its

Left: After a large explosion nearby, probably caused by air or artillery attack, these *Hitlerjugend* panzergrenadiers pick themselves up and advance to contact with the Allied invaders on the outskirts of Caen.

barrage. A fourth Panzer slid sideways into a shell crater and proved useless.

Around the same time, Panzer Meyer spotted 3rd Canadian Division advancing confidently in the direction of Carpiquet airfield, 7km (4½ miles) west of Caen, blithely ignoring 3rd British Division, which should have been protecting its left flank. Unaware of Meyer's hidden vantage point within the Abbey, a Sherman, caught in the German's field glasses, rumbled to a halt a mere 180m (600ft) away. Its commander, standing upright in his turret, lit a cigarette, Meyer's glasses even picking out the man wincing as the smoke was blown into his face. The German ordered the hidden anti-tank guns of *Obersturmbannführer* Wunsche to hold fire until the most favourable moment. The Highlanders of 3rd Canadian Division advanced into the orchards, only to be slaughtered as

the Germans opened fire. Those Canadians following behind began pulling back to the village of Authie.

In a bid to join his men, Meyer quit the Abbey. Seizing his motorcycle, he rode in the direction of a battalion. Suddenly a shell exploded directly in front of him, slicing off the motorcycle's front wheel and catapulting him into the air. When he came to, he was pressed into the heaving ground by the force of the explosions around him. Nearby lay a frightened Canadian pilot, also incapable of movement. German and Canadian stared at one another, frozen. Meyer, with a half-humourous shrug, took advantage of a

Below: A knocked out Sherman provides momentary shelter during the increasingly bitter fighting around Caen for a *Hitlerjugend* forward observer. The soldier is using binoculars to detect any Allied movements.

sudden lull in the bombardment to make good his escape towards the battalion. The Canadian headed in the opposite direction.

HEAVY COST

The awesome cost of the attack was only too apparent to Meyer. The grounds of the abbey were littered with the wounded or dying. Meyer's 2nd Battalion commander had been killed in action, along with most of the company commanders, who had either perished or were wounded severely. Third Battalion had also sustained heavy losses; most of the armour had been wrested from the tank detachment.

An incident during the bitter fighting in the area involved 25th Panzer Grenadier Regiment of the *Hitlerjugend*. A church, known to be housing snipers, was stormed. Here, Emil Werner saw his first dead comrade, Grenadier Ruehl, from the headquarters platoon; he had been shot through the head:

Above: Two *Hitlerjugend* men pose before a disabled Cromwell tank. Although the British tank was a match for the PzKpfw IVs that equipped most of *Hitlerjugend*'s panzer regiment, it was outgunned by their Panthers.

'My section commander was wounded in the arm and had to go to the rear. Grenadier Grosse from Hamburg leapt past me, towards a clump of bushes with his submachine gun at the ready, screaming: "Hands up! Hands up!" Two Englishmen emerged with their hands held high. As far as I know, Grosse got the Iron Cross, Second Class, for this.'

The murderous struggle for Caen continued. General Sir Bernard Montgomery, as commander of Allied land forces, called for a massive air attack, to be followed by a last, desperate, attempt to capture Caen by frontal assault. Operation Charnwood was scheduled for July 8. The city should have been taken on D-Day itself, but the approach to the city was a sticky

fly paper, to which adhered men and supplies, all immobilized and made vulnerable to counterattacks. Furthermore, the Canadians had so far failed to take Carpiquet. Among the Allies, there was now considerable alarm; Winston Churchill, the British Prime Minister, was haunted by memories of the bloody stalemate he had witnessed on the Western Front in World War I. Heavy casualties had been sustained and infantry reserves were being bled. There was another pressing reason for securing the bridgeheads: London was suffering the first of Hitler's V1 flying bombs and it was vital to knock out the launching sites.

Around Cheux, west of Carpiquet, fighting was desperate. For the moment, the units of 12th SS, 21st and *Panzer Lehr* Panzer Divisions seemed impregnable. *SS-Haupsturmführer* Hans Siegel, commander of an SS panzer company, later described how he

Above: *Hitlerjugend* **anti-tank crews – such as the one above in a Normandy hedgerow – inflicted a considerable toll on enemy tanks, particularly when the Allies suffered from a shortage of protecting infantry.**

disposed of numerous enemy tanks in the surrounding countryside, earning himself the Knight's Cross.

'Shell after shell left the barrel of our gun, each one a hit. We fired so fast that the ventilators could hardly cope with the fuming gases...abruptly the ground in front of us appeared to explode – a tank shell fired from the right flank...The lone enemy tank...was 365 metres [1200ft] away. Before we could even swing the gun around to bear, he hit us. Flames blew up around us and escape hatches flew open.'

Siegel's gunner bailed out, his clothes aflame. He was followed by the gun loader, but Siegel himself was unable to get free from the turret hatch. In front of him was the radio operator. With one final effort, Siegel pushed him through the hatch, tumbling after him. Then he was in mid-air, hanging down the tank's side while machine-gun fire rattled against the armour plating. Then he realized that he had neglected to unplug the wireless lead around his neck. After a desperate struggle, he managed to disentangle himself and, on hitting the ground, roll clear, out of the line of fire.

General Geyr von Schweppenburg, commander of Panzer Group West, met with Meyer, and announced a gigantic effort to break through to the

Below: *Hitlerjugend* **panzergrenadiers come under bombardment during their advance north of Caen. South of their position was open tank country, and the division was keen to prevent the Allies breaking through them.**

coast with three armoured divisions. Out of Caen, 21st Panzer would attack on the right with *Hitlerjugend* in the centre and the *Panzer Lehr* Division on the left, near Bayeux. Von Schweppenburg was under no illusions: there could be but one attempt, and it had to succeed. The British and Canadians, however, appeared in front of the German lines and gradually edged the three divisions over on the centre.

PRESSURE

Unrelenting pressure by the Allies forced the Germans to commit units prematurely, taking casualties as a result. But the British were not having things all their own way: there was insufficient infantry to protect the tanks. A particular humiliation was experienced by a leading brigade of 7th Armoured Division. Emerging from a small wood in the area of

Left: The fighting in Normandy was disjointed and sporadic, a pattern only broken when the Allies launched an offensive. Gradually, however, the Germans were pushed backwards as the weight of Allied numbers told.

Above: SS *Kubelwagen*s (the German equivalent of the jeep) make their way carefully through the ruins of a French village. The Allies used heavy bombers several times in Normandy to blast a hole in the German lines.

Villers Bocage, which lay directly west of Caen and the airfield at Carpiquet, it was challenged by a lone Tiger crewed by *Obersturmbannführer* Michael Wittmann and gun-layer *SS-Rottenführer* Wolf. A Cromwell, one of the latest models of British tanks, but still completely out-classed by the excellent German Panthers and Tigers, was the first of a series of blazing wrecks. With the arrival of yet more Tigers, the brigade was soon forced to fall back towards Villers Bocage, a dozen Cromwells seeking to cover the retreat.

Then a shell ripped into the right track of Wittmann's Tiger. From the rubble of wrecked houses, British troops launched their spring-powered anti-tank spigot mortar, the PIAT (Projector, Infantry, Anti-Tank).

The Germans withdrew, satisfied that they had stopped the advance of an entire British brigade.

PROPAGANDA

Even at this stage of the war, the German propaganda machine was tireless, as demonstrated in the lurid style of an SS reporter writing for the magazine *SS-Leitheft:*

'Thousands of aircraft, rolling barrages of the batteries, masked tank attacks hammered them in with bombs and shells. The earth heaved thunderously. An inferno was unleashed. But faith was the strongest support of courage. Smeared with blood, covered with dust, gasping and fighting, doggedly dug in the earth, these youths brought the Anglo-Americans to a halt.'

Right: A *Hitlerjugend* panzergrenadier peers round the corner of a building to check for the enemy, while a Panther tank from the division's panzer regiment waits behind him for the all-clear.

It was an achievement that had its cost. During what he thought was a lull in the fighting, Fritz Witt made for his château headquarters to lunch with *Oberschüze* Hans Matyska, another of the intake from the *Leibstandarte* Division. Then came the roar of 406mm (16in) naval shells from two British battleships stationed off the coast. At first, Witt thought the target was a battery positioned in the Odon valley, to the southeast. He assumed too that this would be the point on which the enemy would concentrate, but then came a second salvo, landing much nearer. Everyone was ordered to take cover in a prepared anti-shrapnel trench, which lay under tall trees behind the house. Witt was the first to leap in. At that moment a shell exploded in the tree tops, sending showers of shrapnel downward. A large piece sliced into Fritz Witt's head. There were further explosions, the shrapnel scattering over the garden and claiming other victims.

NEW COMMANDER

Within half an hour, the Division's Chief of Staff, Herbert Meyer, ordered 'Panzer' Meyer (no relation) to take over the command. For Meyer, an ardent Nazi fuelled with the confidence and arrogance of early battlefield successes, the death of Witt was a bleak inheritance: by 1 July 1944, British VIII Corps had pressed 12th SS Panzer Division back to the western suburbs of Caen, where 26th Panzer Regiment of the *Hitlerjugend* had been reduced to mere battalion strength, its tank, auxiliary and engineer components all but annihilated. In the north, the Panzers of the division lacked petrol, ammunition and equipment.

A flak battery held on precariously to Carpiquet, whose airfield had become the last bastion of the Caen defences. Time and again, Meyer requested permission to pull back to the river line that ran through the centre, and which was shorter and thus easier to defend. This proved fruitless, drawing only

the familiar mantra: 'The Führer Order demands not a yard of ground be yielded'.

The frail forces at the disposal of the Germans had as opponents the Canadian 8th Infantry Brigade, together with a battalion of the Royal Winnipeg Rifles, buttressed by tanks of the Fort Garry Horse and armour of the British 79th Armoured Division. They also had to contend with the concentrated firepower of 428 guns and warships, including 406mm (16in) guns of the battleship *Rodney* and the monitor *Robert*'s 381mm (15in) guns. Against these were pitted some 50 SS panzergrenadiers, supported by *Obersturmbannführer* Max Wunsche's Tigers. Concealed in an aircraft hangar, they were soon facing forces of the Royal Winnipeg battal-

ion. The latter were confronted by the fierce fanaticism of a mere 150 teenagers, who advanced from the hangar, crouching low and firing from the hip. Caught momentarily off guard, the Canadians were beaten back. They did eventually secure Carpiquet, but this was by no means a walkover. The men of the Royal Winnipegs had to endure a cascade of flame throwers and there was unexpectedly strong tank support. Furthermore, the place was bristling with solidly built underground blockhouses bisected by a network of passages. By the end of the day, 4 July, 117 Canadians were dead and 260 wounded.

Matters were different on the right of Kurt Meyer's front. There he was depending on the 16th Luftwaffe Field Division. This, in itself, was an illustration of just how desperate things had become for the Germans. These men were ex-pilots and gun crews, who were ignorant of infantry warfare and thus proved to be a serious liability in battle.

Montgomery's next initiative was Operation Goodwood, actioned on July 18 and involving all four British and Canadian corps in Normandy. The resources of German intelligence warned of a major operation pending. Sepp Dietrich, though, used less sophisticated methods. Using a trick picked up on the Russian front, he put his ear to the ground and detected the rumble of oncoming British tanks. The Allies were faced with formidable defences, consisting

of four belts of natural and man-made obstacles and a reserve of tanks. The open, rolling agricultural land appeared peaceful, but its dominating ridges concealed 88mm (3.45in) flak/anti-tank guns. The villages were also formidable centres of defence. Matters were scarcely helped, either, by network of hills and narrow valleys; dominating the northern ridge was the acutely steep scrub cover of Mont Pichon, 29km (18 miles) southwest of the town. Further south, a clutch of Panthers and Tigers waited out of artillery range. Another worry for the Allies was the Orne bridgehead, rapidly becoming a log jam; there were only six narrow river crossings for around 8000 vehicles.

BOMBARDMENT

General Miles Dempsey, commanding 2nd British Army, to which the Canadians belonged, turned to the Royal Air Force to overcome the determined resistance of the SS. This began with the guns of the battleship *Rodney* directing 29 shells at a distance of 228km (142 miles) on the key hill at Point 64, where the roads from Epron and Lebisey converged before running down to Caen. Next came over 450 four-engined heavy bombers, dropping a load of 2560 tons.

To the east, near the village of Emieville, Lieutenant Freiherr von Rosen, with his Tiger company, recalled later that he had found himself in hell:

'I am still astonished that I ever survived...It was next to impossible to see anything as so much dirt had been stirred up by the explosions...impossible to hear anything because of the unceasing crashing...so nerve-shattering we could not think.'

By the end of this hellish assault, 50 men of the company had committed suicide and another was later sent to a mental institution.

The pressure on Caen was unrelenting. Soon the town was being held on the right by an infantry

Left: The *Panzerfaust* was a single-shot anti-tank grenade launcher, the forerunner of anti-tank missiles used by modern armies today. Although only a short-range weapon, it was capable of knocking out any Allied tank.

division and scatterings of *Hitlerjugend* panzergrenadiers. The youngsters fought with a fierceness that astonished even the forces of another single-minded *Waffen-SS* panzer division, *Das Reich,* which was in action alongside. One *Das Reich* man, Wolfgang Filor, later recalled having an American tank full in his sights. He was about to knock it out when he saw a *Hitlerjugend* soldier raise his *Panzerfaust* – anti-tank rocket — as a signal to hold fire. Within seconds, the youth fired the *Panzerfaust,* and the tank blew up, taking him with it. Such gestures proved pointless when seen against the achievement of a single Canadian 17-pounder anti-tank battery, which alone destroyed 13 enemy tanks.

Elsewhere, the German defenders refused to be dislodged, fully obedient to Hitler, who had insisted that 'Caen is to be defended to the last shot.' Although bruised and battered, 12th SS Panzer Division *Hitlerjugend* held firm on Hill 112, southwest of Caen. To the northeast lay the extensive reaches of the Carpiquet aerodrome; Caen itself was positioned to the east; and to the south there was a commanding view across the Orne – the flat, featureless Caen–Falaise plain.

An attempt to dislodge the Germans from this commanding height was made in Operation Jupiter by the British 43rd (Wessex) Infantry Division. The spearhead of the advance was by men of the Duke of Cornwall's Light Infantry, which was virtually annihilated by the German Tigers, who held out steadfastly for more than two weeks, thereby blocking a natural route towards the more open country around Falaise. One survivor, Lance Corporal Gordon Mucklow, recalled, 'All hell broke loose, red hot bullets were sizzling in the earth inches from our helmets.' Described in one account as 'a bloody quagmire', Hill 112 remained impregnable until the Tigers fell victim to the rockets of Typhoon fighter bombers.

There followed an artillery bombardment, most intense around the villages of Cuverville and Demouville, to the east of Caen. Dietrich sent a Panzer reserve to the area of Bourguebus, where the tanks knocked out a succession of Shermans –

another corner of Normandy had become a killing ground. In Caen itself, the British and Canadians were tying down even more German forces to the east. As a result, the Americans further west faced understrength infantry units backed by just two panzer formations.

All of which came as no surprise to Sepp Dietrich, Hitler's hard-drinking Bavarian gladiator. From the very start, he had expressed his reservations about the entire Normandy campaign. Earlier, he had complained to Rommel that he was 'being bled and getting nowhere'. When ordered by Rommel to attack, he demanded, 'With what? We need another eight or ten divisions in a day or two, or we are finished.' 'Panzer' Meyer came to the same conclusion: 'The Division's casualties are considerable. In this situation, one can only calculate on the Division being completely wiped out.' Ignoring Hitler's direct orders, he pulled his troops back to to the south bank of the Orne river. Later, he wrote:

'The fresh blooming faces of a few weeks ago have become hollowed out and grey; the boys' eyes are already dead....We were meant to die at Caen.'

Among the pursuing Canadians was Duncan Kyle from Ontario:

'Suddenly we were in a savage fight. We opened up with Brens and rifles. I swung my rifle slightly to the right. I was staring into the face of a blond SS soldier. He was on his belly, facing me. Our eyes locked. I squeezed the trigger a split second after he raised himself on his elbows. The .303 slug caught him just below the throat. The impact lifted his body straight into my face. A pool of blood was forming on the pavement under his chest. He looked sleepy, his head nodding. He was still on his elbows and was waving his hands...He was dying. I think about him often. When he saw me take aim, he had started waving his hands in a gesture of surrender.'

On 9 July, British and Canadian troops took Caen, which had been reduced to rubble by a bombardment of 2500 tons. The only area fortunate enough to survive was around the majestic Abbaye-aux-Hommes, which had become a refugee for the homeless. The full force of air bombardment had fallen on the *Hitlerjugend*, some of whose strongpoints of resistance held until burnt out by the flame-throwers of British tanks. But to keep Caen was out of the question; on 8 July, Rommel took the decision to prepare for evacuation of the town. The order was given that all heavy weapons be moved across the Orne river, which flowed through the city.

LOSSES

The 12th SS Panzer Division *Hitlerjugend* had lost 20 medium tanks, several 88mm (3.45in) guns, its entire stock of anti-tank guns and a high percentage of its troops. In all, Rommel reckoned that overall losses were the equivalent of four battalions. On the morning of 9 July, British and Canadian troops entered Caen from the flanks and reached the Orne, whose bridges were either destroyed or blocked by rubble. The frontline soldiers of 12th SS were by now totally worn out: in one bunker on the edge of the town, they had fallen into a deep sleep, their officers obliged to take over the guard duties. Stragglers who staggered into the bunker collapsed to the floor. But there was to be no respite. The youths were prodded awake and ordered to the eastern bank of the Orne, to bolster an already hopeless defence and to join others who had somehow reached there ahead of them. As recorded in Hubert Meyer's history of the 12th SS Panzer Division, *Rottenführer* Paul Hinsberger wrote:

'We were 36 men. Ahead of us stood a Canadian vehicle column, the men gathered around fires. In the vicinity of the previous trench of 11 Company, of which no one was left, we lost five men...We reached the rear positions outside Caen with 31 men.'

It was clear that Hitler, as supreme commander, was utterly indifferent to the blood-letting. This was demonstrated in a letter dated 21 July 1944, from Heinrich Himmler to the Reich Labour Leader Konstantin Hierl:

'Having learnt that the SS Panzer Division *Hitlerjugend* has already lost 3000 men, the Führer asked me what replacements I had...I informed the Führer that I would get into contact with the *Reichsjugendführer* with the object of getting him to

provide, once again, a fairly large number of volunteers for the SS Panzer Division *Hitlerjugend*. The *Reichsjugendführer* promised me 6000 volunteers... The *Hitlerjugend* Division now has casualties of 6000, including 2000 dead. The painful truth is that, at the lowest estimate, one third of the wounded are amputees, since most of the injuries have been caused by artillery and dive bombing. We must see to it that these divisions do not bleed to death totally, since they are...in the truest sense decisive for the war.'

By 26 July, the forces of General Omar Bradley had penetrated the German front at St Lô, south west of Caen on the River Vire. Four days later, the newly

Above: With the exception of a few unrepentant fanatics, surrender came as a blessed relief for many in the *Hitlerjugend*. Aside from some rare instances of summary shootings, most were treated humanely by their captors.

formed Third Army of General George Patton had reached Avranches, thus opening the way to Brittany and the Loire in the south. All that was left of the German Army in Normandy was locked in a narrow area which became known as the Argentan–Falaise gap, the term describing the distance that separated American and Canadian forces. These allies now sought to close the bloody inferno that would become the Falaise pocket.

CHAPTER FIVE

FALAISE

After the fall of Caen, the narrow pocket south of Falaise was described by Eisenhower as 'one of the greatest killing grounds of any of the war areas'. The battle-stained survivors of the division were sucked into this hell on earth, in which hundreds would lose their lives.

From early on, the campaign in Normandy had caused a crop of anxieties for the Americans and these had centred on the Contentin peninsula. The problems could be traced right from the time of the conception of Operation Cobra, which had been suggested to Montgomery as commander of the Allied land forces by General Omar Bradley. The aim of Cobra had been to trap the bulk of the Germans in the area south of Cherbourg where the last German strongpoints had surrendered on 29 June. Here the LXXXIV Corps of Major General Dietrich von Choltitz would be pinned against the coast. At the same time there had been a proposed strike south west towards Coutances, launched from the road between St Lô and Periers. Then would come the surge south from the region of La Haye-du-Puits, squeezing the Germans into a pocket.

However progress by the Americans had been slow, and worsening weather brought about the postponement of Cobra. One of the results of this was an unexpected disaster. The decision to reschedule had been taken after aircraft had taken off on a

Left: The strain of battle clearly shows on the face of *SS-Sturmbannführer* Hans Waldmüller of the 25th Panzer Grenadier Regiment in his command post near Cambes on the outskirts of Caen.

supporting bombing raid from England. It was assumed by the crews that Cobra was safely underway and the area clear of US forces, High explosives from 70 heavy bombers and medium bombers arriving in two waves were dropped on American forces with heavy casualties, including civilian observers. Among the dead was Lt General Lesley J McNair, the former commander of Army Ground Forces and the highest-ranking American to die in the north-west Europe campaign. It was swiftly realised that if news of his death leaked out, the disposition of American forces would become known to the Germans; McNair was the commander of the phantom First Army Group, having replaced Patton in that role. The burial of McNair was thus carried out secretly amid a security clamp-down.

HARD FIGHTING

The German defenders at first had faced demoralised and depleted American forces during a ground assault on 25 July. But the Americans eventually rallied, driving south west from the St Lô to Periers road. During this progress the Panzer *Lehr* Division had been subjected to a massive attack and had reeled under more than 500 tonnes of high explosives and napalm. The division's commander, General Fritz Bayerlein, recorded:

Above: This Panzer IV displays an impressive number of killer rings on its 75mm (2.95in) gun. Although produced in greater volume than any other type during the war, its numbers were dwindling fast thanks to Allied aircraft.

Right: While one of their number keeps watch, these two halftrack crew men hastily dig defensive positions in which to spend the night. The risk of attack meant that every precaution had to be taken, even behind the lines.

'By noon nothing was visible but dust and smoke. My front lines looked like the face of the moon and at least 70 per cent of my troops were out of action – dead, wounded, crazed or numbed.'

Hitler, lost in his maps and charts, never seemed to appreciate the dire position the Germans were in. Those at the sharp end were more realistic. A 'Most Secret' report from Rommel, forwarded to Hitler by von Kluge, Commander-in-Chief West, was blunt:

'The position on the Normandy front is daily becoming more difficult and is reaching crisis proportions... The infantry divisions now arriving are without combat experience, have low establishments of artillery and of anti-tank weapons. They also lack close combat anti-tank weapons and are unable to offer determined resistance after they have been subjected to drum fire for many hours. Experience has shown that even the best units are shattered by the enemy's material superiority and by their losses in men and material.'

HEAVY LOSSES

Rommel spelt out those losses: '... about 97,000 men (of whom 2350 were officers)... that is a daily wastage of between 2500 and 3000 men. Our material losses have also been high and have only been replaced in part, of about 225 panzers lost we have received only 17 replacements... The Army is fighting heroically everywhere but the unequal combat is nearing its end...'

For the Americans, the focus was on blasting open a hole in the German lines which would make a drive on the Seine possible. This would necessitate the capture of the town of Falaise, lying south east of Caen. To achieve this, Eisenhower and Bradley worked out a strategy for encirclement, aiming to trap the German defenders, preventing their withdrawal and forcing their surrender. To achieve this Bradley unleashed units of the Third Army under General Patton. His forces included Major General Jacques Leclerc's French 2nd Armoured Division, positioned far to the south at Le Mans, which would now make for Argentan in the north. Here Anglo–Canadian forces, attacking from Caen and later Falaise, would create a vast, yawning pocket to trap the Germans. Falaise as yet had not been taken and, to do so, First Canadian or Second British Army would be required to thrust to

the south east and capture Trun, the point for a link up with Patton's advance.

However German resistance was too strong for this to be achieved and the attack ground to a halt, less than halfway to Falaise. The Germans had taken heavy casualties: 85th Division barely existed and *Hitlerjugend* had lost all but 15 of its tanks. Three battalions of 25th Panzer Grenadier Regiment had shrunk to two battle groups, *Kampfgruppen* Waldmüller and Krause. Two weak gun and one rocket battalion was the sole content of artillery. As well as standard reconnaissance troops, the divisional headquarters company consisted of engineers, anti-tank, flak groups and two platoons of grenadiers. After the fall of Caen the division had been withdrawn from the line for a rest, but the respite had been brief and the division had been sent back to continue fighting until relieved. It came straight into the path of the Canadians, together with Polish tank crews, who were thrusting southwards in two operations, codenamed 'Totalize' and 'Tractable'.

Panzer Meyer, suffering the effects of a head wound after dive-bombers had attacked his car, faced the stark reality that if he did not make the best of his division's resources, however depleted, the Allies would be through Falaise, and the German armies in the west would be trapped beyond rescue. The date of 14 August 1944 was set for Operation Tractable, the drive into Falaise itself, and simultaneously a westward thrust towards Paris. The plans were compromised, however, by a Canadian officer who blundered into the German lines and was killed. On his body the

Germans found plans for the Tractable attack, enabling the Germans to strengthen their defences.

The opposition *Hitlerjugend* faced was the full force of 1st Canadian Army including the 51st Highland Division, 4th Canadian Armoured Division, two Canadian armoured brigades and the 2nd Canadian Infantry Division. In addition, it was planned for II Canadian Corps to sweep southwards at night, smashing an enemy which would already have been weakened by relentless aerial bombardment. The SS grenadiers met this threat by spacing out their motorized convoys, making themselves harder targets for Allied airpower. The Germans advanced with

Left: A field dressing is being applied quickly to a wounded *Hitlerjugend* youth by his comrades. Soldiers with far more severe wounds fought on against the Allies in Normandy, unable or unwilling to desert their position.

Below: The ever-closing jaws of the Falaise pocket. The remnants of the division fought hard to keep the two Allied armies apart, so that as many Germans could escape as possible, but thousands died in the battle.

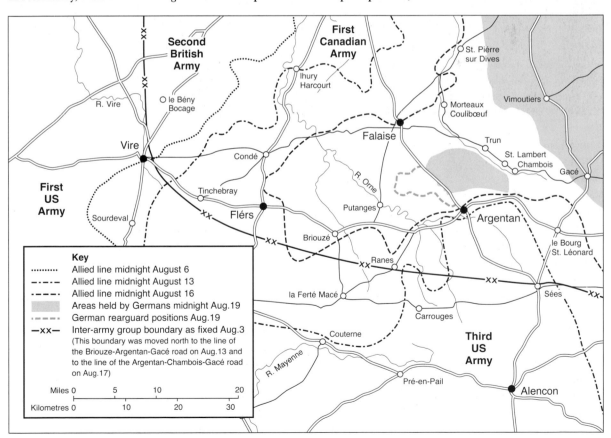

determination, driving through the Cinglais woods, via St Laurent and from there into the Grimbosq woods, heading for the sector of the Allied bridgehead which had been established across the Orne river. The division's advance was stemmed by a solid wall of opposition which meant that the personnel carriers and tanks could progress no further. The SS grenadiers dismounted and fanned out, beating their way forward, firing all the while and forcing the British infantry back, and eventually out of the woods altogether. Under fresh bombardment the panzergrenadiers fell back, only to advance again through the village of Grimbosq, beyond which lay the bridgehead. However the attackers were too weak and, at an enormous cost in dead and wounded, could only reduce the bridgehead's extent.

Meanwhile, I SS Panzer Corps, which had been seeking to hold the British at Conde, 26km (16 miles) south-west of Falaise, was all but spent, its ammunition exhausted. The Free French lurked menacingly behind, poised for the big sweep from around Ecouche. This was the French citizen army, the men of the Maquis, sniping and rounding up stragglers who were cut down without mercy, as well as mopping up in the wake of the Allied advance and exercising to the full their talent and expertise for sabotage. This would have the effect of rapidly narrowing the gap forming the sole escape route from the pocket.

CINTHEAUX

Panzer Meyer witnessed another instance of just how grim the situation had become. In a drive to the tactically important village of Cintheaux, lying a mere 1000m (1094yds) from the Canadian positions, he encountered a single anti-tank platoon covering the Caen–Falaise highway down which men of the 89th Division were fleeing. In his book *Grenadier*, Meyer wrote that he himself was unarmed except for a carbine and was accompanied only by his driver:

'I am seeing German soldiers running away for the first time during these long, gruesome, murderous years. They are unresponsive. They have been through hellfire and stumble past us with fear in their eyes. I look at the leaderless groups in fascination. My uniform sticks to my body, the fear of responsibility making me break out in a sweat… I jump out of the car and stand alone in the middle of road, talking to my fleeing comrades. They are startled and stop… They recognise me, turn around, and wave to their comrades to come and organise the defence on the line to Cintheaux.'

All was still not lost for the Germans, however. A bid was made by Lieutenant General Simonds, commander of II Canadian Corps, to seize Hill 195, west of the main road and situated half-way between Cintheaux and Falaise. The result was humiliating for the Allies; the column lost its way in the dark and had to withstand repeated counter attacks from the *Hitlerjugend* Division at the cost of 45 tanks. A later attempt secured the hill and the Germans were driven back some 14km (9 miles). But the objective had not been achieved. There was a further setback when two columns of tanks with infantry of 4th Canadian and 1st Polish Armoured Divisions advanced down both sides of the Caen–Falaise road under the cloak of air strikes. German resistance proved too great and the attack stalled. General Patton had already boasted that his American formations could have easily entered Falaise and closed the gap, but this move had been opposed because of the possibility of collision with British forces. The Germans' escape route to the east remained open.

In the evening of 15 August, the Royal Winnipeg Rifles and the 2nd Armoured Brigade faced infantry and tanks at the village of Soulagny which was the launching point for the attack on a point designated Hill 168, secured after prolonged fighting, costing a Canadian battalion 37 killed and 93 wounded. Reinforcements were called up and the attack resumed from another hill with gains made deep into the village.

The *Hitlerjugend* was in danger of being surrounded but a Tiger tank was on hand to relieve the division. The tank closed in on six Shermans, driving slowly line astern, covering the German foxholes with constant fire against which the panzergrenadiers had no defence. What happened next was a neat illustration of a tactic often employed by Tigers, which was to fire first at the leading tank and then the one in the rear.

Above: Two *Hitlerjugend* panzergrenadiers move from their dug-in position, armed with MP 40 submachine guns. The high grass provided a degree of cover from Allied artillery observers and fighter-bombers.

Without a pause the Tiger turned its full fury on the remaining four Shermans, only to find that all at once it was facing another column of armoured personnel carriers. The crew of the German tank briefly thought the new arrivals to be grenadiers, until the afternoon sun picked out the clear white stars on their vehicles. The Americans stood no chance with a quick succession of explosive shells and machine gun salvoes. The personnel carriers had been fully loaded; the column sat burning and smoking. The village of Soulagny had become a killing ground.

Five days later, another attempt was made – a mad charge in which 250 Canadians and Poles attacked the pocket head on. Sergeant Leo Gariepy, a French-Canadian tank commander, recalled:

'It was a beautiful sunny day and this great column of armour moved through fields of waving grain like

Above: A *Hitlerjugend* gun crew duck for cover as an Allied naval shell lands in the distance. For much of the Normandy campaign the Allies were able to call on naval fire support to suppress any German strongpoints.

eerie avenging centaurs straight from hell... Speed, nothing but speed, and on we went, crashing through obstacles at 20 to 25mph [32–40 km/h].'

The charge took the Canadians and Poles to the outskirts of Falaise. The German defence of the town was in the hands of *Kampfgruppe* Krause of the *Hitlerjugend,* under the command of *Sturmbannführer* Bernhard Krause. Strong defence points were set up along the ancient city wall and faced north and north west. For the SS, the battle began to the west of the Falaise road during the evening of 6 August 1944. The British 59th Division and 34th Tank Brigade established a bridgehead across the Orne

river above Thury-Harcourt, with the intention of turning the flank of the German troops in the Falaise sector. *Kampfgruppe* Krause was detached and marshalled with 89th Division in a bid to destroy the British lodgement. But the 89th lacked armoured support and heavy anti-tank guns. The sole artillery it could boast was horse-drawn, and there was no mobile reserve.

During the fighting, *Kampfgruppe* Krause became isolated and an order to withdraw was slow to reach it. After an exchange in which ten Canadians and four panzergrenadiers were killed, the men of the *Hitlerjugend* withdrew to the ancient, thick-walled *Ecole Superieure de Jeunes Filles*. Here between 50 and 60 panzergrenadiers holed up, secure for a while with sufficient weapons and provisions. From the building's top floor they had, for the moment at least, a commanding position on the south side of the town and the main route of the Allied advance. The Canadians brought up their tanks and there was an attempt by troops to push into the building which was repulsed with heavy casualties. In his account of the exchanges, Hubert Meyer wrote:

'After nightfall, two young grenadiers managed to make their way to the German troops outside of Falaise. Since no-one had wanted to leave their comrades the two had been selected by drawing lots. They reported to the Divisional commander that the surrounded men… would resist to the last.'

Within the school, the number of wounded among the SS defenders was mounting. The final attack involved 100 men of the Canadian Fusiliers Mount Royal were supported by anti-tank guns and Bren carriers. Eventually the school was torched. The Canadian brigade's report stated:

'The building was occupied by members of 12 SS who fought staunchly to the end. With the exception of four, who were able to flee into the sector of the South Saskatchewan Regiment, no prisoners were taken. At 05:00 hours we found several piles of dead Germans in the vicinity of the building, and burnt corpses inside the house.'

Many Germans made good their escape following the fall of Falaise on 16 August 1944; about 40,000 men had fled eastwards across the Dives in the face of artillery shells and the pursuit of Allied troops. The Canadians who had approached the suburbs along the Route Nationale had a hard time of it, taking the full brunt of fire from an anti-tank gun and machine guns positioned on a bridge. *Sturmmann* Heinrich Bassenauer, who had taken the place of a wounded anti-tank gunner, made for the top floor of a carpenter's shop near the bridge where he succeeded in knocking out a Canadian tank which had emerged from behind a bend in the street. The machine gun nest was spotted, and Bassenauer attempted to edge away but was caught in a shower of shrapnel. Together with a colleague, he was on his way to the field hospital when suddenly he saw two burning German tanks to the right of the road. However the ambulance was allowed to pass through the fighting unharmed, the Canadians contenting themselves with a burst of machine fire that did no damage to the vehicle.

The Falaise pocket had become the target of an epic dive bombing offensive with squadrons of rocket-firing RAF Typhoons and USAAF Thunderbolts pounding the area, while there was strafing of a small triangle formed by Falaise and, to the east, the villages of Trun and Chambois. The fighter-bombers attacked columns in a similar way to a German Tiger: seal off a column's front and rear by dropping a few bombs with pinpoint accuracy, imprisoning the enemy on a narrow stretch of road or lane to be despatched at leisure. Transports were thus frequently jammed four abreast on a road while the fighter-bombers roared into the attack. One Allied artillery observer described such scenes as 'a gunner's paradise… Everyone took advantage of it'. On the ground, all was panic and chaos. Cars, heavily laden with officers' gear, sounded their horns in the desperate bid to clear a path through the shattered lorries while cannon shells slammed into the ammunition trucks.

PAUL HAUSSER

At this time Panzer Meyer made contact with a former comrade, *SS-Obergruppenführer* Paul Hausser, commander of Seventh Army, who was subordinate to Field Marshal Walther Model. The latter had replaced Field Marshal von Kluge as Commander-in-Chief West. Model had thus become the third holder of the post in less than six weeks. Von Kluge had previously taken over from Field Marshal Gerd von Rundstedt, who had been in poor health and accused by Hitler of defeatism. The reign of von Kluge, widely known as 'clever Hans' – a play on the German '*kluge* Hans' – did not last long. On 15 August, at the height of the Falaise onslaught, he had lost contact with his headquarters for several hours. Hitler, still smarting from the attempt on his life the previous month in the July Bomb Plot, was convinced von Kluge had been negotiating with the Allies. Ordered to report personally to the Führer and believing he was a marked man, von Kluge took his own life with a dose of cyanide.

By this stage of the war Model had become a legend as the so-called 'Saviour of the Eastern Front', where he had proved adept at forming a firm and cohesive battle line following even the most disastrous breakthrough. Although his loyalty to Hitler was beyond doubt, this did not stop him blithely ignoring what he regarded as impossible orders, acting first and obtaining authorization later. To the consternation of the more subservient generals and Nazi Party members, he could be fearlessly outspoken when it came to denouncing any interference with his generalship. On one occasion, he had stared coldly through his trademark monocle, daring to interrupt Hitler by curtly demanding: 'Who commands Ninth Army, my Führer, you or I?' Model may have been determined to put the German defences on a sound footing, but the situation he found in Normandy was to defeat even him.

The pocket which contained the German forces was shrinking by the hour. The combined British, Canadian and American strengths were pushing the German remnants eastwards. In the areas of Chambois and Trun the Allied pincers had all but closed and it was up to Model to hold them open. But how? Hitler could gaze mesmerized at his maps at Supreme Command headquarters which showed a comfortable array of flags representing divisions, corps and armies within the pocket. But what the maps did not show was the total absence of any command structure for these contingents, which meant there was no way reliefs or supplies could be secured. Model's inheritance was a shambles. Movement became increasingly hazardous. *Hitlerjugend* fought desperately to hold onto a small village near a network of minor roads through which units might be able to retreat. But at the approach to Chambois and Trun the wreckage of tanks and other vehicles jammed the roads. Self-propelled guns, armoured troop carriers and artillery drawn by vehicles and

Left: A knocked-out PzKpfw IV tank being inspected by a couple of British paratroops. The division lost most of its armoured strength in the chaos of the Falaise pocket – on 1 September 1944 it possessed only 10 panzers.

horses had been abandoned. Infantry wandered like zombies amid the stench of death. Caught up in the fighting inevitably were the innocent: French civilians seeking to escape from wholesale slaughter.

The Allied air raids had been merciless but during the cold and misty morning of Friday 18 August there was a respite. Visibility was bad and the congested columns could not be targeted. But then came the news that the Canadians had captured Trun. Orders were issued to the 2nd and 9th SS Divisions: 'II SS Panzer Corps will attack and will break open the ring between Trun and Chambois'. But crossing points across the Dives were soon a rarity. It soon became apparent to Panzer Meyer that a link up with other forces was mere fantasy; all the bridges across the Dives were in enemy hands. There was a flicker of hope when heavy gunfire was heard from the direction of St Lambert-sur-Dives. For six precious hours the Germans managed to keep one road east open but the northern half of St Lambert was held by the Canadians. One squadron of the 29th Canadian Armoured Reconnaissance Regiment and one company of the Argyll and Sutherland Highlanders of Canada with 175 men, 15 tanks and 4 anti-tank guns resisted any assault and eventually orders were given for St Lambert to be shelled. Canadian guns continued their fire on those units crossing the Dives to the east bank.

The Australian journalist and broadcaster Chester Wilmot in his widely acclaimed book *The Struggle For Europe* wrote:

'... Several close columns of horse-drawn transport were caught in bombardments as they approached the bridge. The horses stampeded. Careering through hedges and fences, the terrified animals plunged down the steep river bank, dragging their wagons and gun carriages after them. Soon the ravine was choked with wreckage and with the bodies of men and horses, the dead and wounded lying together in gruesome heaps.'

A stone bridge and a light bridge behind St Lambert and the Moissy ford were the only remaining crossing points which could be taken by those escaping across the Dives. Attempts were made to construct further emergency bridges but these only served to obstruct progress as did a narrow road running through the village of Tournai-sur-Dives, forming a bottleneck inevitably choked with the bodies of the dead.

Among those who made a bid to escape was *Untersturmführer* Herbert Walther, a member of the *Hitlerjugend* Division who had joined the Hitler Youth at 11 years old and, at 18, had volunteered for the *Waffen-SS*. He fought in the battle for Caen, winning the Iron Cross First Class. He recalled:

'My driver was burning. I had a bullet through my arm. I jumped onto a railway track and ran. They were firing down the embankment and I was hit in the leg. I made 100 metres [109yds], then it was if I was hit in the back of the neck with a big hammer. A bullet had gone in beneath the ear and come out through a cheek. I was choking in blood. There were two Americans looking down at me and two French soldiers who wanted to finish me off.'

One of the Americans bandaged his leg, from which no less than 13 bullets were later removed. Then, lying on the bonnet of a jeep, Walther was driven away to captivity.

HOLD THE POCKET

In overall command of LXXXIV Corps, which included 12th SS Division *Hitlerjugend*, was Lt-General Otto Elfeldt, whose orders were to hold the shoulders of the pocket open until paratroopers had forced a passage enabling as many as possible to escape. All unusable vehicles and useless equipment was to be jettisoned during the breakout. The light from burning lorries blazed the trail to the narrow corridor. The noise from tank tracks, exploding artillery shells, and machine guns was deafening, orchestrated by the screams of the wounded and the dying.

In their book, *The Killing Ground: The Battle of the Falaise Gap*, James Lucas and James Barker quote an account of the retreat from an unidentified source:

'... There was the terrible tiredness, a sort of lead-en-footed sensation and, fighting through waves of exhaustion, we would find ourselves still marching, still putting one foot in front of the other and still

Above: Yet more digging for this panzergrenadier, seeking protection from Allied bombardments and air attack. Infantrymen of both sides spent hours digging positions before moving to a new location and starting again.

keeping in touch with the man in front and the man behind. There was, I suppose, food but I cannot remember regular meals or even if we ate at all. Just exhaustion so great that men would lean against the trees or walls and fall asleep on the spot. And yet each man carried his weapon, ammunition and grenades... Wherever one looked there were bodies. The stench was appalling, for the fields were filled also with the bodies of artillery horses and civilian cattle. There were columns of burnt out trucks and in the cabs of some, the incinerated bodies of the drivers. There were corpses along the roads, in the ditches, some of them blown into the tree tops. The dead bodies lying on the roads were often rolled over by the tanks and crushed under the tracks.'

The *Hitlerjugend* group, its numbers lessening all the time, moved forward from its position in the woods, making for the west of the Trun–Chambois road manned by machine guns that swept their fire along with the cannon of the tanks. Panzer Meyer wrote his own account:

'Death shadows us at every step. We are lying as if on a salver in full view and range of the 4th Canadian and 1st Polish Divisions' guns. It is impossible to miss. By chance we find the Seventh Army's battle headquarters in an orchard one kilometre [two-thirds of a mile] south west of Trun. The commanding general and I go to army HQ. The roads cannot be traversed as they are blocked by motorized and horse-drawn supply columns. Each and every shell explodes ammunition trucks and destroys vehicles. We run, stumble and jump by degrees towards headquarters...'

Members of *Kampfgruppe* Krause had a significant role in countering the Allied drive to break down the shoulders of the pocket, Divisional headquarters at Necy were overwhelmed; SS survivors teamed up with *Kampfgruppe* Krause in a new position which lay to the south of the railway line. The pressure from Allied fire was becoming more than the panzergrenadiers could bear. However, Max Wünsche arrived with a panzer detachment. A participant recorded:

'They had carried out battles against overwhelming odds so many times that the situation was normal to them and their tactics were those we had used on the Eastern Front. The panzer would be revved up and would roar forward with all guns blazing. We knew that the Allies felt a sense of inferiority when faced by Tigers and we depended a lot on this moral effect. Wünsche's group roared away and soon were lost in clouds of dust and smoke. They charged into the enemy who had broken through and not one panzer returned. Wünsche, who had been awarded the Oak Leaves [to his Knight's Cross] only a week before, was badly wounded and captured.'

Unfortunately for the Germans, the effectiveness of the panzer charge was shortlived, and its protagonists easily disposed of.

LUCKY FEW

Among those who did manage to escape before the corridor through St Lambert was finally closed was Paul Hausser, who, badly wounded, was taken out in a personnel carrier. His rescuer, who informed Hausser that they were outside the area of encirclement, received no thanks whatever. Indeed, Hubert Meyer relates in his history of 12th SS Panzer Division that Hausser had stormed: 'I will bring you before a court martial. How could you transport a supreme commander from the field of battle without his agreement?' Meyer states, however, that no subsequent court martial was held.

As for Panzer Meyer, he crossed the Dives with about 200 of his group, reaching an area which had

been commandeered as a casualty collecting point where scores of wounded lay in the open, often next to their dead comrades. There were those who volunteered to join Meyer's march, but he allowed only those who were fit and armed to do so. Besides these, though, were plenty of soldiers waving makeshift white flags of surrender. No one could rely on the protection of tanks. Those in the pocket had been unable to cross the Dives since its bed was too deep. It was merely a question of moving from cover to cover with a pistol in hand. Ditches were choked with dead bodies of men crushed by tanks and looted vehicles stood in the fields and hedges.

At one point Meyer and his group found themselves between two Allied tanks some 150m (164yds) apart, their fire raking the line:

'Suddenly there is a Sherman tank 30 metres [33yds] to our right. Hubert Meyer yells to me. I would have run straight into its gun muzzle. We run, leaping and jumping over the ground like weasels, the hedges protecting us from being seen. I cannot go on anymore. The last few days have taken too much out of me.'

Eventually Meyer's group was obliged to split up to avoid capture. From then on progress meant stumbling through ditches that were choked with the dead, their bodies crushed by overrunning tanks, while looted vehicles stood in the fields and behind hedges. A total of 600 panzergrenadiers and a handful of vehicles advanced for days to the next great river line, the Meuse, to find that Belgian partisans had mined the roads. The bodies of those who had fallen victims were abandoned; it was obvious that pursuit by the Americans could not long be delayed.

Meyer and the almost totally exhausted remnants of the division managed to hold out for a further 36 hours around the Belgian village of Durnal. But eventually the strength of a powerful group of Belgian partisans proved too much. Meyer, now holder of the

Right: The body of a *Hitlerjugend* soldier lies before a half track, part of a convoy that appears to have fallen victim to an Allied fighter-bomber. The division was decimated in the fighting for the Falaise pocket.

Swords to his Knight's Cross, was captured and eventually handed over to the Canadians for a singularly traumatic period as prisoner of war.

A last attempt by II SS Panzer Corps was made on August 21 to relieve those forces which remained in the pocket. Nothing, however, could dislodge the Polish forces hanging on to a ridge lying to the north of Chambois. On the following day the corps joined Model's forces in a general retreat. They left behind 44 tanks, self-propelled guns and armoured vehicles, 2447 lorries and cars and 252 towed guns, along with the cadavers of an estimated 8000 horses.

The Canadian 4th Armoured Division, which had moved to Vimoutiers, in the northeast, was badly mauled by a large German armoured column. Nonetheless it had the advantage of a good defensive position and formidable firepower, and the enemy's tanks were soon burning and close-packed infantry were shut down. These were men on a hiding to nothing. Wild-eyed and battle-stained, the SS stumbled forward to surrender, a number claiming to be Poles or Czechs who had been forced to fight for the Germans. There were claims that members of *Hitlerjugend* in the column, fearful of reprisals, had discarded their tell-tale SS uniforms and had donned those snatched from *Wehrmacht* corpses. Indeed, In the general mêlée, there were reports of Canadians mowing down prisoners with machine gun fire, claiming they were responding in kind to actions by the *Hitlerjugend*.

IKE'S VIEW

Few who had been at Falaise disputed the later judgment of General Eisenhower:

'The battlefield at Falaise was unquestionably one of the greatest killing grounds of any of the war areas.

Roads, highways and fields were so choked with destroyed equipment and with dead men and animals that passage through the area was extremely difficult. Forty-eight hours after the closing of the gap, I was conducted through it on foot to encounter scenes that could be described only by Dante. It was literally possible to walk for hundreds of yards at a time, stepping on nothing but dead and decaying flesh.'

The figure of some 10,000 Germans slaughtered during the six days of their bid to escape through the gap took no account of those who were also killed before they reached the Seine; total casualties were reckoned to be 45,000. Eight divisions of infantry and two panzer divisions were captured virtually intact. In Normandy as a whole, total German casualties were put at over 450,000. A total of 43 German divisions had been destroyed or put out of action, leaving aside garrisons trapped in the Brittany ports and the Channel Islands. The armies that Hitler had thrown into the campaign had been completely routed. Patton's progress towards the German frontier was unopposed.

Any sane evaluation of Germany's fortunes following Caen and Falaise would have concluded that the war was as good as lost. Indeed, von Rundstedt had urged surrender and a bid for peace, a move which had led to his removal.

During their retreat, elements of the *Hitlerjugend* became further involved in fighting between the Touques and Seine rivers, an area where it had been intended they should be refitted. With considerable understatement, Hubert Meyer recorded:

'Since personnel replacement arrived only in insufficient numbers, and material replacement hardly at all, it had been impossible to set up combat-ready units again.'

Supplies could only reach crucial areas aboard wheeled carts, pulled by horses at their own pace. Dispersed motorized *Wehrmacht Kampfgruppen* were

Left: Prisoners captured in the Falaise pocket after it was sealed, including a number of *Waffen-SS* soldiers. On the left is an *SS-Hauptscharführer* with an Iron Cross and on the right a *Luftwaffe* prisoner.

also pressed into the service of the surviving field battalions. By now any slowing effect on the Allied forces' advance caused by the frantic German defenders was minimal.

At the beginning of October, the whole division was moved into the Lower Saxony, southern Oldenburg and northern Westphalia areas for refitting, urged on by a direct order from the Führer that all refits were to be completed by the last day of October. Their preparation was somewhat frustrated when the division had to release some of its forces for brief front-line action in the Reichswald near Kleve on the Lower Rhine. In the meantime, to mark their battle record, the two panzergrenadier regiments of *Hitlerjugend* were presented by Artur Axmann with sleeve bands carrying the inscription '*Hitlerjugend*'.

The resumption of refitting was by no means greeted with universal enthusiasm, and there were those at this stage of the war prepared to give up the struggle, particularly in the knowledge that the division as such had ceased to exist and was little more than a *Kampfgruppe* given what was essentially an emergency 'fire brigade' role. There was also widespread bitter feeling that the withdrawal order from the Falaise Gap had been issued too late, causing needless casualties.

Last Throw

Even now, though, the war had not done with them. As the German armies in Normandy were streaming to the borders of the Reich in defeat, Adolf Hitler was nurturing a dream, a last throw of the dice: to force a breakthrough in the forest of the Ardennes to the Meuse, then sweep north for the seizure of Antwerp. By doing so, he hoped to force the Allies to negotiate an end to the war. Even now there remained a hard core of fanatics in the *Hitlerjugend* willing to follow him to the end.

Right: The looted body of a panzergrenadier, still clutching a spare MG 42 barrel case, in a Normandy hedgerow. The *Hitlerjugend* Division had paid a heavy price for its defiance of the Allied onslaught.

CHAPTER SIX

ARDENNES

Convinced of his strategic genius, in December 1944 Hitler decided to re-run the *Wehrmacht*'s triumphant 1940 progress through the Ardennes. However the division was no longer the force it had once been, consisting of 15 and 16 year-olds and SS training school recruits.

Normandy had proved not only to be the testing ground of the *Hitlerjugend* Division but its grave. When, on 4 September 1944, the division crossed the Meuse River in the course of its retreat to the Reich, it was down to precisely 600 men. There were no tanks and the artillery had no ammunition, a state of affairs which had led Field Marshal von Rundstedt to comment: 'It is a pity that this faithful youth is sacrificed in a hopeless situation.' At this stage, *Hitlerjugend* was made up of recruits scraped from the bottom of the barrel, but the hunt was on for still more.

Withdrawal to the static defences of the *Westwall*, or 'Siegfried Line' on the borders of the Reich was seemingly the only option left for the Germans. However, Hitler intended to use its protection as the springboard for his latest offensive. His enthusiasm was fuelled by the belief that the Western alliance was coming apart at the seams, confidently arguing that the Anglo–Canadians were in favour of quitting the southern Netherlands and that the Americans would be forced to turn their attention to the burgeoning threat from the Japanese. Once opposition in the West had

Left: The Sixth SS Panzer Army – which included the Hitlerjugend *Division – was given the task of forming the main assault unit for the Ardennes offensive. Here a soldier observes American positions before the attack.*

been annihilated, so went the argument, it would then be time to face the Red Army at full strength.

NEW OFFENSIVE

In late August 1944, Hitler confided to a select group that he envisaged launching a campaign during November which would be aided immeasurably by the likely bad weather, which would seriously impede any attacks by the Allied air forces. The area in which Hitler pinned his faith was the remote semi-mountainous region of the Belgian Ardennes. In shape, the Ardennes represented a large isosceles triangle with an 128km (80 mile) base along the front, extending from a northern point near the town of Eupen in Belgium to the area of Luxembourg city in the south. It was a sector which had brought the Reich sensational success during the summer of 1940, when it had been thought impassable for mechanized armies. The German armour's drive through the region in a *Sichelschnitt* (scythe stroke) was a complete surprise to the Allies. In two short weeks the British had been pushed back to the beaches and cut off from the rest of France, while the Maginot line was outflanked and rendered irrelevant. Hitler hoped that he could repeat such success with a similarly bold stroke now.

The plan was that the proposed onslaught would begin with a long bombardment. Infantry would then advance along a 97km (60 mile) front between Monschau, 25km (16 miles) south east of Aachen, and Echternach in Luxembourg. This would shatter the American defences and allow the German panzers to breakthrough in two waves. The first would be through the woods and hills of the Ardennes, with the aim of seizing bridges across the Meuse River between Liège and Lamur. Next, the second wave would pass through to take the port of Antwerp, cutting off the Anglo–Canadian Twenty-First Army Group and the left wing of the US Twelfth Army Group from the remainder of the Allied formations in France.

For the most part, the terrain, covered with networks of thick forest, was also made up of ridges, plateaux and valleys. Deep ravines alternated with heath, bogs, narrow winding trails and trackless woodland. The forest areas served as a blessing to the German attackers, as accurate Allied air reconnaissance became difficult. The dense forests of the Eifel region inside Germany, the assembly point for the forces to be used in the offensive, provided a ready cloak of secrecy against prying Allied pilots.

Hitler declared that his contingents of SS were to be grouped together as Sixth SS Panzer Army which would supply *SS-Oberstgruppenführer* Sepp Dietrich with four panzer and five infantry divisions. The American line from Monschau to the Losheim Gap in the south was known by German High Command to be lightly held. The initial breakthrough would be entrusted to the infantry divisions and then the initiative would pass to the panzer divisions, in particular the 1st SS Panzer Division *Leibstandarte Adolf Hitler*. The intention was to strike out across the Meuse River and thus reach Antwerp. Three of Dietrich's infantry divisions were assigned to punch an opening in the American front.

Hitlerjugend, with a new commander, *Brigadeführer* Fritz Krämer, replacing the captured Panzer Meyer, would be assigned to the north, tasked with overrunning US positions on the long rise of the Elsenborn

Right: The crew of a Panzer IV chat for the benefit of the camera while waiting for the start of the offensive in late 1944. The poor weather kept the much-feared Allied fighter-bombers grounded.

Above: The human cost of the battle was high. Many of the new recruits to the *Hitlerjugend* division were insufficiently trained, which helps explain the relatively poor performance of the division in the offensive.

Right: A map showing the area of operation for the *Hitlerjugend* Division and the simultaneous advance of *Kampfgruppe* Peiper. The division encountered stiff resistance on Eisenborn ridge.

Ridge. It was further envisaged that the *Hitlerjugend* would swing northwest through the town of Spa to the Meuse bridges, near Liège. The *Leibstandarte*, under *SS-Oberführer* Wilhelm Mohnke, would take the southerly route, a network of less-than-perfect roads beginning near Lanzerath and leading to the Meuse bridge at Huy, some 80km (50 miles) away.

Hitler's grandiose plans need to be seen in the context of the prevailing state of German forces. In five years of war, Germany had lost virtually 3,750,000 million men. Hitherto Russia, the Balkans, Finland and France had served as a bottomless pit for raw materials, together with such supplies of iron ore as could be prized out of neutral Sweden. Such

resources were no longer available. Some 28 divisions and two brigades held in reserve were capable of deployment for use in the offensive – 275,000 men, 1900 heavy artillery pieces and 950 armoured vehicles. But these could go into battle only at the expense of defence in the east, which was crumbling day by day as the Red Army advanced.

In addition, virtually the whole of northern France apart from the Channel ports had been liberated. US Sixth Army Group was in hot pursuit of the German Nineteenth Army up through Central France. Though Walter Model, as Commander in the West and of Army Group B, had been able to put new fire into the belly of a disillusioned and disheartened *Wehrmacht* and SS, it was obvious that the task of command in the West required exclusive attention. On 1 September, von Rundstedt was summoned to the *Führerhauptquartier* and given back his old job. There were those who believed that his state of health made this a poor decision, recalling that the veteran commander had earlier suffered a heart attack. A British Twenty-First Army Group Intelligence Review put its finger on the uncomfortable truth:

'The reappointment is interesting as exhibiting muddle and desperation; but it doesn't really make much difference. The task of Commander-in-Chief has degenerated into that of local Chief-of-Staff to Hitler and liable to dismissal as much as for carrying out quaint orders as for protesting against them.'

Preparations for the assault were carried out with the utmost secrecy. A good deal of this, of course, was for military and strategic reasons, but Hitler was even

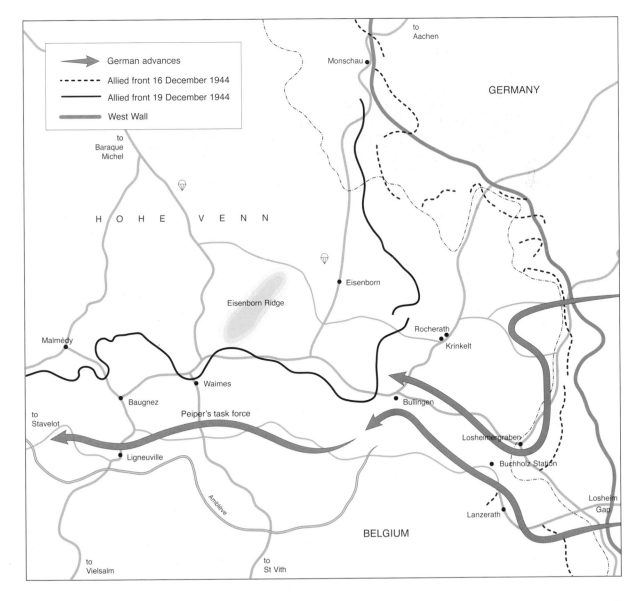

cagey in his dealings with von Rundstedt. Both men disliked each other – to a contemptuous von Rundstedt the Führer was 'that Bohemian corporal', while Hitler regarded him as a stiff-necked Prussian reactionary. At a meeting in the *Wolfschanze* (Wolf's Lair), his East Prussian headquarters, Hitler deliberately assumed an air of diffidence and respect. Von Rundstedt was asked to defend the front along the *Westwall* for as long as possible. Hitler then went on blandly to stress that, of course, there was insufficient strength to mount any new offensive. His next move was to order four SS panzer divisions to be refitted without telling von Rundstedt why, and to ensure that the latest tanks coming off the assembly lines would be accorded Western Front priority.

IMPRACTICAL SCHEME

Von Rundstedt though,was not deceived for long. His opinion of Hitler's scheme was expressed forcibly to Model: 'Antwerp! If we reach the Meuse, we should go down on our knees and thank God; let alone trying to reach Antwerp!' The sheer impracticality of Hitler's scheme boiled down to lack of personnel and armour. To his allied interrogators at the war's end, von Rundstedt admitted: '… no soldier really believed that the aim of reaching Antwerp was practical. But I knew by now that it was impossible to protest to Hitler about the impossibility of anything.' Model, also an anathema to Hitler, was blunter: 'The damned thing hasn't a leg to stand on.'

In fact, von Rundstedt had suggested a more modest plan, which was known as the 'Little Solution' (*kleine Losung*). This was to scale down the offensive to an attempt to excise the American forces which had pushed beyond Aachen to the Roer river. The suggestion was rejected by Hitler out of hand. From that point onwards, von Rundstedt's distanced himself from proceedings as far as he could, passing the time reading novels and copiously imbibing brandy.

Right: A PzKpfw VI Tiger II (known as the 'King Tiger' or 'Royal Tiger') of Sixth SS Panzer Army advancing through the Ardennes carrying paratroopers. The Tiger II, though powerful, was relatively slow and unreliable.

Yet, even though Hitler's proposals were beyond reason, von Rundstedt adhered unswervingly to orders in a true Prussian tradition to what he considered was his path of duty. A bare two months before the launch of the Ardennes offensive he had trumpeted to his men:

'You have brought the enemy to a halt at the gates of the Reich. But we will shortly go over to new super

attacks. I expect you to defend Germany's sacred soil with all your strength and to the very last… Soldiers of the western front! Every attempt of the enemy to break into our Fatherland will fail because of our unshakeable bearing. Heil the Führer!'

Concealed by Allied air surveillance, the narrow mist-bound valleys and thick forests of the Eifel on

through his penetration to the suburbs of Moscow three years before.

The greatest asset possessed by the Germans was the complacency of their opponents. Despite the fact that reports of activity in the area of the Ardennes had inevitably reached Allied Intelligence, Allied commanders fed Eisenhower with the misguided belief that the Germans were merely concentrating their reserve formations against a possible American breakthrough. By general consensus, a major German offensive operation was out of the question. To the 83,000 American troops there, spread thinly over Eisenhower's 1600km (1000 mile) front line, it was ideal for rest and relaxation. Occasionally there would be exchanges with isolated pockets of Wehrmacht troops, but otherwise the war seemed a remote, far-off affair.

MASSIVE RESOURCES

None of this took into account that Germany was still able, despite the immense losses it had suffered, to muster 10 million men in uniform with 7.5 million in the army, to say nothing of the *Waffen-SS* whose *Hitlerjugend* Division could still field a hard core of fanatics. The Germans' weakness was their lack of hard battlefield experience, particularly in units where sailors and airmen had been turned into infantry. As Dietrich commented ruefully to his Allied inquisitors after the war: 'The Führer was all for the offensive thrust and there was nothing to be done.'

Hitler, despite his declining physical powers, drew on seemingly boundless reserves of energy to plan the forthcoming assault. A blizzard of orders descended on subordinates for the planning of the initial artillery bombardment. At the same time, he immersed himself in detail, tirelessly inspecting plans for tanks that would be required to spread grit on icy roads. On 12 December, he delivered a long lecture in an underground bunker at Zeigenberg. Here a host of generals, brought from Koblenz during the night by a bus which

the German side of the Ardennes were host to a formidable force. Here were two Panzer Armies, Sixth SS commanded by Sepp Dietrich in the north and Fifth in the south. The latter would be driven with pugnacious ruthlessness by the diminutive Hasso-Eccard von Manteuffel, one of the best of Germany younger generals, who had earned his spurs

had twisted and turned and gone back on its tracks to deceive them about the route they were taking, were relieved of their side arms and briefcases. What none of them could have failed to notice, however, was Hitler's conspicuous physical decline. Before them was a hunched figure, with a pale and puffy countenance, his hands trembling, and one arm kept rigidly on the table so that it would not be seen to twitch.

The voice, however, proved as strong as ever, its old mesmeric power intact. His listeners were obliged to submit first to a diatribe on the sterling example of how a steadfast Frederick the Great had, against all advice, refused to surrender in 1761, and had emerged victorious. This was followed by a rambling harangue against both Britain – 'a dying empire' – and America. Hitler maintained that there was no common accord between the two: 'A few well-struck blows and this artificial common front could come crashing down at any moment.' But there were indications that Hitler was not unaware of the perils faced by his forces, since he concluded his address by saying: 'Gentlemen, if our breakthrough via Liège to Antwerp is not successful, we will be approaching an end to the war which will be extremely bloody. Time is not working for us, but against us. This is really the last opportunity to turn the fate of this war in our favour. I thank you, gentlemen.'

Considerable courage was later shown by Hugo Kraas, who, at another conference, voiced his concerns directly to Hitler about the lack of personnel within the division, the inadequate level of training and the shortage of weapons, vehicles and equipment. Hubert Meyer in *The History of 12.SS Panzer Division Hitlerjugend* recalled that Sepp Dietrich, sitting next to Kraas, had tried in vain to silence the other man by kicking him on the shin, but Hitler had calmly asked Kraas to voice his concerns.

In the end, though, it made no difference. After several postponements, the attack went ahead at 05:30 hours on 16 December, heralded by a 20-minute

Right: Although this Panther appears to be making good progress, many of the roads in the Ardennes were narrow and treacherous, and it did not take much for a traffic jam to build up, compromising the German schedule.

Above: These men of Sixth SS Panzer Army are helping themselves to rations, fuel and anything else they can salvage from this captured American position. American rations were far superior to standard German fare.

Right: A shot from a German propaganda film, subsequently captured by the Allies, shows members of Sixth SS Panzer Army posing by a burning American half-track in an captured convoy.

barrage of searchlights, piercing the thick winter mists. From these, shock troops overwhelmed American divisions in the frontline. In the American rear, German infiltrators in American uniforms cut telephone wires and spread confusion. Operation *Wacht am Rhein* (destined to be known more prosaically as 'the Battle of the Bulge') was underway. The opening drive of the battle shattered two American divisions spread along the Schnee Eifel ridge in the north and along the Our river in the south, and it was four days before the American front could be reestablished with any effectiveness. Dietrich, concealing his personal misgivings about the operation from his men, was committed to getting to the Meuse river within two days.

The main attack by the armour would be in two echelons, led by I SS Panzer Corps, with the *Leibstandarte* on the left and *Hitlerjugend* on the right with II SS Panzer Corps behind. From the start, there were severe problems. To keep to the punishing schedule the tanks of I SS Panzer Corps needed access to sufficient petrol for five refuellings, giving a range of up to 272km (170 miles). On the day of the attack they could only secure two refills. To camouflage his intentions, Hitler had forbidden the creation of fuel dumps close to the line; even more crucially, he had made no allowances for the difficult terrain or very bad weather.

The commander of I SS Panzer Corps' spearhead was 29-year-old *SS-Obersturmbannführer* 'Jochen' Peiper,

head of his own *Kampfgruppe* (battle group) and formerly an adjutant to Heinrich Himmler. Peiper already had a reputation for combining a daredevil *élan* and total ruthlessness in battle with military efficiency of the highest order. His track record of service in Poland, France, Greece and Russia was impressive and he had been awarded the Oakleaves to his Knight's Cross of the Iron Cross.

On the eve of the Ardennes offensive, Peiper had awaited a fresh assignment without any idea what it might be, since Sixth SS Panzer Army had taken the most stringent measures to conceal its move into the new assembly area. Then he was quizzed by Fritz Krämer, Chief of Staff of Sixth Panzer Army, who had asked him what he thought of an offensive which would cut through the notoriously bad terrain of the Eifel area in winter. Peiper had also been asked how long he considered it would take for an armoured

regiment to travel 80km (50 miles) under the severest winter conditions. His reply had been to take out one of his own Panthers and drive it 80km (50 miles) over the narrow, winding roads. The next morning he had reported to Krämer that the local roads 'are broad only for bicycles'. From now on Pieper knew which way the wind was blowing.

Peiper's *Kampfgruppe* possessed a strength of around 5000 men, comprising 1st Panzer Battalion of 22nd SS Panzer Regiment, an SS-Reconnaissance Battalion, artillery, anti-aircraft guns and ancillary personnel and material. This force was to be kept perpetually on the move during the offensive, with all threats to flanks being ignored. Across a narrow region that was rich in bends and distinctly unfriendly to armoured vehicles, the route to Antwerp would take Peiper west through the village of Honsfeld and on to Baugnez. This would be followed by a progress south

Left: A *Sturmgeschütz* (assault gun) or StuG of Sixth SS Panzer Army with accompanying SdKfz 251 half track. Assault guns, essentially tanks with no turret and a fixed gun, were cheaper and quicker to manufacture.

Above: Standing in front of their half track, *Hitlerjugend* soldiers discuss the fate of the American prisoners they have just taken. Two of the *Waffen-SS* men are carrying *Panzerfaust* anti-tank rockets.

to Ligneuville, with a westward strike to Stavelot on the Amblève river, arriving finally at Trois Ponts, the key river crossing in the Amblève valley. From then on progress should be easier: a road which was excellent for armour would lead on to Antwerp.

FUEL PROBLEMS

All this was only possible, of course, if fuel supplies held up and all too soon there were signs that they would not. However, Peiper had been briefed that there was an Allied fuel dump situated in the market square of the town of Büllingen, northwest of Baugnez. This was not on the defined route for his attack, but he did not hesitate to peel off and secure what he needed, despite opposition from dug-in American tanks. Peiper's move to Büllingen did not, however, find

favour with *Hitlerjugend* since the paved surface road which Peiper had taken to reach the town itself, lay directly on Rollbahn C, the main route assigned to the 12th SS Panzer Division. This had been of little moment to Peiper with his single-minded intention of getting his tanks to the Meuse river, but the resulting tangle of traffic worsened the German delays. *Hitlerjugend*'s next task was to clear the way through Büllingen and widen the gap in the American lines, thus facilitating the progress of I SS Panzer Corps. Speed was imperative, especially as the Americans had briefly recaptured the town.

During the night of 18 December, the first elements of *Hitlerjugend* gathered to attack a ridge near Butgen-bach, a cluster of large houses and farm buildings which were part of an estate that lay beyond Büllingen.

Above: A Panther column in the Ardennes is passed by a *Kubelwagen*. Delays to the German advance were caused by a severe lack of fuel, and the Germans were not able to capture as much American petrol as they had hoped.

Right: A map showing the full extent of the German offensive. The *Hitlerjugend* Division, a shadow of its former self, had nowhere near the same impact as its sister division, the *Leibstandarte Adolf Hitler*.

Inside Büllingen itself, some 20 *Hitlerjugend* soldiers, quartered inside the house of farmer Albert Kohnenmerger, slept in the cellars. They had already experienced something of the wrath of American artillery and for this group at least, aged for the most part between 15 and 17 years old, there was no wish to repeat the experience. Kohnenmerger was with them when the orders came that they were to return to duty. He noticed that many of them were weeping, as they gathered their gear to move out into the cold night, to a rendezvous with death.

At first the *Hitlerjugend* managed to tear vast gaps in the American line but, even so, only a few panzers emerged through the storm of exploding shells, driving along the line through the cloying mud, raking the American foxholes with machine-gun fire and wiping out enemy positions. All the while American artillery rained down upon the men of the division, an indication of the advantage the Allies enjoyed as artillery support was a commodity that the panzers conspicuously lacked. The Americans also had a major advantage in terms of numbers. The German armour rumbled towards buildings where the houses and barns formed an American command post. Two German tanks were disabled, but one managed to escape. The daily situation report of I SS Panzer Corps was terse: '*Angriff 12. SS-Panzer-Division und 12. Volks-Grenadier-Division auf drang nicht durch.*' (The attack by *Hitlerjugend* did not break through).

In the Krinkelt-Rocherath area, which lay to the north-east of Butgenbach, *Hitlerjugend* suffered particularly heavy casualties. American Captain Charles Macdonald described German infantry storming his lines, exchanging volley after volley of fire:

'Germans fell left and right. The few rounds of artillery we did succeed in bringing down caught the attackers in the draw to our front, and we could hear their screams of pain when the small arms fire would slacken. But still they came! Seven times they came, and seven times they were greeted by a hail of small arms fire and hand grenades that sent them reeling down the hill, leaving behind a growing pile of dead and wounded.'

An account by a German company commander gave a graphic picture of the plight of the tank crews: 'On the right there was a row of tall spruces running parallel with the direction we were taking. These stood on the highest point of the meadow, with a slope leading gently up to them, but with nothing to be seen on the far side. It was in this area of dead

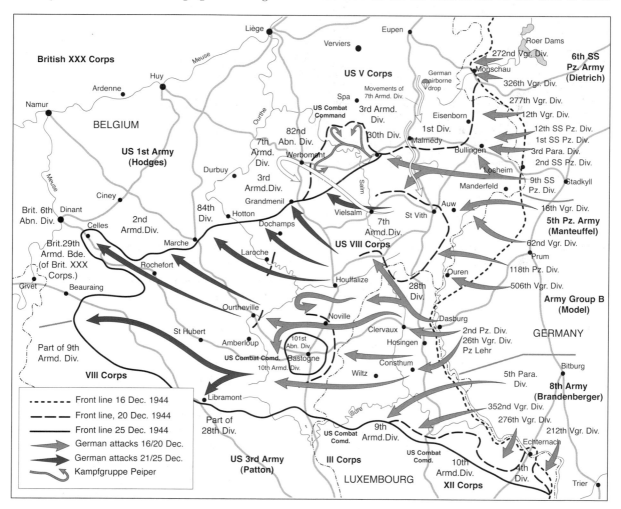

ground that the objective of our attack had to be lying. There were still some clouds of mist which had spread away. Instinctively, as if in response to an order, all the turrets swung round towards the row of trees on our right flank. There had been no firing yet but the silence seemed ominous. As we moved on, we sent one or two bursts into the trees with our machine guns, by way of initiating the fight against an imaginary enemy. We sensed, however, that there was an enemy somewhere out there, excellently camouflaged, and sitting watching us through the eye-pieces of his anti-tank gun sights…'

'*SS-Untersturmführer* Schittenhelm had just reached the projecting border of the woods when a spout of flame shot out from the rear of tank, as if it came from a spectral hand. The Panzer was hidden by thick, black smoke mushrooming up – two men managed to get out of it.'

'*Hauptmann* Hils gave the order to get ready for action. He was standing in his turret and studying his map to make an exact check on his position. Then he fired a flare to indicate the direction to be taken by the attack. The flare died away over the downward sloping terrain. Now we waited for the "*Marsch! Marsch!*" order to attack. As nothing happened, I took another look at his tank. The turret was burning and there was no sign of *Hauptmann* Hils any more. The crew were abandoning the tank: I could recognise the driver, *SS-Unterscharführer* Bunke, and likewise the radio operator whose name I didn't know. I unfortunately had to accept that the rest of the crew, which as well as Hauptmann Hils included the gunner Lorentzen and the gunlayer Krieg, had become casualties.'

The meadow in which the action was taking place was now ploughed up and a number of tanks had perished under direct hits. *SS-Untersturmführer* Engel had pulled back his tank for extra protection, but this did not stop his vehicle from attracting bazooka fire. From his new position he was able to make a report over the radio, estimating that there were at least two anti-tank guns in the row of spruces that had originally aroused the Germans' suspicion.

Effective direct fire was not an option. Instead a quick succession of high-explosive shells were directed into the treetops. To Engel's satisfaction, he saw a number of Americans running away from blazing wrecks in the direction of the woods. He swung the tank towards the row of trees and opened fire. But his satisfaction was brief; the panzer bore the full brunt of an artillery bombardment.

UNDER FIRE

Under fire in the same area was *Sturmmann* Heinz Muller of 5 Panzer Company with his Panzer IVs. He had mounted an attack near a housing estate. Hubert Meyer in his history of the division gives Muller's account:

'The Grenadiers, however, were stalled and unable to keep pace with us because of the heavy artillery fire. During that attack, one of *Oberscharführer* Kretzschmer's tracks was blown off. We took one of his crew into our vehicle and continued the attack with six men in the Panzer. We were knocked out close to the first houses of the estate. Then we tried to reach our own lines along the road, without success. After moving back toward the spot of the estate where we had been knocked out, we managed to be spotted by our company, and split up into the remaining vehicles.'

The Americans were having their own problems, however, as one eyewitness attested: 'Aid stations overflowing, wounded men being evacuated by Jeep, truck, ambulance, anything that could roll, walking wounded, prisoners going back under guard, trucks rolling up to the front with ammunition and supplies and firing at the same time at low-flying airplanes. Vehicles off the road, mired in mud or slush or damaged by gunfire, only to be manhandled off the traffic lane to open the road; signal men trying to string wire to elements to cut off or to repair lines which were being shot out as fast as they were put in.'

Butgenbach was not taken by the Germans on that day, but they had no intention of giving up. At 06:30 hours on 22 December, *Kampfgruppe* Kuhlmann tried

Right: As the poor weather continued and the German advance ground to a halt, many of the Sixth SS Panzer Army took refuge from the cold and enemy artillery in hastily constructed shelters.

again, this time from a position further west. But the outcome was merely a series of inconclusive engagements. The much depleted ranks of panzergrenadiers pulled back and several panzers were left behind for the maintenance units to do what they could for them.

Willi Fischer, whose tank had been disabled at Krinkelt, to the northeast of Butgenbach, had some happier moments:

'... We were able to clean up a completely abandoned food depot, after which the company later enjoyed many goodies. We had become self-sufficient. Over the Christmas period we moved into rooms in a peasant's house as the cold in the Panzer had become unbearable. Our rest period during those days was marred by constant mortar fire. With great difficulty, and after all the efforts of two 18-ton tractors had

failed, we were towed into the workshops by an armoured recovery vehicle.'

Heinz Linke, a commander whose panzer had lost a track on a mine during the attack on Butgenbach, was forced to take shelter time and again while attempts were made by the recovery vehicle to couple his tank which stuck obstinately in the frozen mud. Although this was eventually achieved, it was in the face of American firepower at its most vicious outside Büllingen. Linke related: 'The recovery vehicle burst into flames and it wasn't long before we caught it too. All of us except *SS-Untersturmführer* Jansen were out in the open. He got a splinter in his backside but could still walk. In no time at all both Panzers were blazing.'

On 18 December, *Hitlerjugend* and 12 Volksgrenadier Division succeeded eventually in retaking Büllingen, after Peiper had passed through, only to find that they had to redouble their efforts to hold on

Left: Typified by this *Waffen-SS* MG 42 machine gunner steadfast among ruined buildings, many fanatical Germans, and notably the *Hitlerjugend*, conducted a desperate defence as the Allies began to regain lost ground.

Above: The rare sight of a PzKpfw IV tank moving in daylight on an Ardennes road in early January 1945, after the offensive had effectively ended and the Allies were slowly recapturing territory from the Germans.

to the town. The chronic lack of fuel continued to be a source of anxiety for commanders at every level. Fritz Krämer later wrote:

'Often the fuel consumption was much higher than anticipated because of the bad road conditions. When some of the supplies arrived at all in the main line of resistance, it was due to the untiring activity of the truck drivers and the energy of the staff of the supply services.'

All reserves were near exhaustion, and those that were available came from supporting units, notably artillery, who were made to sacrifice their own supplies in favour of the armoured spearheads.

Due to faulty radio communication, contact with Jochen Peiper was intermittent. It had become increasingly clear that the *Kampfgruppe* needed maximum support if there was to be any prospect of Peiper reaching the Meuse river. Krämer was ordered to disentangle his *Hitlerjugend* youths from Butgenbach, moving them south in order to enlarge the salient made by Peiper. However, the roads had proved impassable – hence the decision was taken to try once again to seize Butgenbach. But all efforts were frustrated, due to the cloying mud as much as tenacious American resistance. Success was thus denied to Peiper, whose Tiger tanks, by Saturday 23 December, were dug in at the village of La Gleize, which the Americans had ringed in anticipation of an attack by fighter bombers. The bulk of *Kampfgruppe* Peiper was forced into the village's cellars. Christmas was marked by American tanks and infantry braving a solid wall of dug-in panzers and anti-tank guns, followed by a German withdrawal of 800 men, all that remained from the 5000 who had gone in just a week before.

Back in Germany, the Nazi newsreels of December 1944 were speaking only of certain victory with shots of beaming *Hitlerjugend* on their way to battle, while the Reich radio proclaimed the rapid collapse of 'Allied resistance'. The experience of 17-year-old Johannes Schroder was lying in a dugout when he heard the deafening noise of tank engines. 'There were 14 of us against 100 tanks. What hope did we have? Near me, one man dropped after another. The guy next to me in the trench got a bullet in the neck and I was shot in the head.' He was discovered eventually by American medical orderlies; his comrades, thinking him dead, had abandoned him.

TURNING POINT

The crucial turning point in the Ardennes had been the arrival of General Patton's US Third Army from

Below: German prisoners and their American escorts wait for a path to be cleared along an impassable stretch of road. The weather and the state of the roads were among the reasons given by Hitler for the attack's failure.

the south. His main objective was the relief of the market town of Bastogne with its vital road centre. The failure to capture the town had severely delayed the German bid to strike for the Meuse river. Now events elsewhere, most notably the Red Army's new offensive on the Vistula river, caused Hitler to divert troops from the Western front to meet the threat. The Allies seized the advantage: despite poor weather conditions, they eventually managed to take Baraque de Fraiture on the Liège–Bastogne road. Patton then renewed his attack northwards from Bastogne and Echternach. Model, faced with entrapment at Houffalize, northeast of Bastogne, by the twin Allied pincers, at last received permission to withdraw.

It was the beginning of the end for the Germans in the Ardennes; the Bulge was squeezed out of existence. There were an estimated 120,000 casualties among the *Wehrmacht* alone. The *Luftwaffe* was all but a spent force. About 15,000 casualties had been inflicted on the Allies, whose operations in the Ruhr and the Saar had only been postponed for – at most – six weeks. True, Germany still had some five million troops in the field. However, in 1944 alone 106 German divisions were destroyed – three more than had been mobilized at the outbreak of war. Hitler was still convinced that Germany was capable of fighting a major war and strong enough to create fresh effective divisions. The strength of this fallacy was outlined after the war by Albert Speer, the armaments minister: 'New divisions were formed in great numbers, equipped with new weapons and sent to the front without any experience or training, while at the same time the good, battle-hardened units bled to death because they were given no replacement weapons or personnel.'

As for the Hitler Youth, members by now were either being automatically conscripted at the age of 16 into 12th SS Panzer Division *Hitlerjugend,* or were mustered into pretentiously termed *Volksgrenadier* (peoples' grenadier) divisions. These were hastily assembled replacement units, the detritus of shattered divisions and depot staff. Among those in the *Hitlerjugend* Division who fought in the Ardennes was Gunther Munz. He had originally been an ordinary *Wehrmacht* volunteer and had lost a leg on Christmas Day, vainly trying to stem the flow of blood by holding his trouser leg tight at the bottom: '… We were told: "It's your age group that will turn things round, you've been called upon to do it." That's when I learnt to cry.'

While General Omar Bradley's Twelfth Army was ordered to capture a bridgehead over the Elbe river, on 1 April 1945 at 13:00 hours, US First and Ninth Armies sealed the Ruhr. Both armies advanced on a two-corps front, the Ninth with one corps on each side of the autobahn in the Teutoburger Wald, sited near the large industrial town of Bielefeld. Once through the forest, the Ninth was to cross the river Weser, the last water barrier before the Elbe.

Lieutenant General Karl Becher, the newly appointed commander of the German front, had, at most, 7000 men to make up eight or nine divisions, consisting for the most part of lower grade soldiers and even two 'ear battalions' (men suffering from hearing deficiencies). Otherwise there were *Volksturm* units of Home Guard, and men from the SS training division stationed at the nearby infantry school at Senne.

Becher's forces took the full power of the American assault on the night of 2–3 April 1945. After the initial air bombardment, the Ninth Army attacked along the entire XII and XIV Corps area. Light resistance was encountered north of the autobahn. By now the Allies only needed to conduct sporadic mopping-up operations. A firm front by the Germans was out of the question; small pockets of guerrilla warfare was all that was possible.

Although by that late stage the *Hitlerjugend* had been shifted to the east, it was still a force with which to reckon. Those who had fought in the Ardennes from the beginning had learnt their lessons well. Their technique was to allow American armour to penetrate their lines, then wait for the approach of the infantry, inching cautiously through the wooden heights. Then the young Germans attacked, firing indiscriminately into knots of American infantry, and clinging to their positions to the last man.

Between Detmold and Bielefeld, opposition to the American advance had come not just from the *Hitlerjugend* Division, but from youth who had been mustered into battle with the barest of military training.

In one instance, Lieutenant Roland Kolb of the US 84th Division had noted that his men were up against an 'artillery unit' manned by boys of 12 and under who 'rather than surrender fought until killed'. All were mown down. In addition, young GIs reported that members of the *Hitlerjugend* were butchering captured American troops with an orgy of slaughter around Eisenborn ridge. The GIs responded in kind.

FINAL THROES

The reality was that the German offensive in the Ardennes was long over. However, even now Nazi propaganda strove untiringly to hold out the prospect of final victory. In his Christmas 1944 address, Josef Göbbels declared: 'We have put a year behind us that is unique in German history. In this war the German people are showing a degree of moral stamina which can only earn admiration. It is the guarantee of the victory which will eventually come.'

General Patton characteristically riposted with: 'I think the Hun has shot his wad.' It was a view to which even Hitler had eventually to subscribe. He conceded to *Generalmajor* Wolfgang Thomale, his Inspector of Motor Transport, that the offensive had failed. The Führer admitted that: 'Only the first wave of the 12th SS Panzer Division's tanks were in action, while behind them there was an enormous convoy jammed solid, so that they could go neither forward nor back. Finally, not even petrol could get through. Everything was stationary, and the tanks' engines were merely idling. To keep the men warm, the engines were run all night. This created enormous petrol requirements.'

Typically, the Führer had ignored his own fundamental miscalculation in undertaking the offensive in the first place; 'the horrendously bad roads' had been mainly to blame, along with traffic congestion. Yet faced with the virtual collapse of his Western front, he did not hesitate to sacrifice yet more of the *Hitlerjugend* on the altar of his ambitions.

Left: Bereft of any equipment and paraded by their American captors, these two *Hitlerjugend* soldiers are displayed in their tattered uniforms. The trousers of the youth on the right of the picture are secured by string.

CHAPTER SEVEN

HUNGARY

With the Red Army virtually unstoppable in its advance west, Hitler's main focus became Hungary's precious oil resources. The Führer called on the *Hitlerjugend* Division once more as he planned another audacious offensive to recapture Budapest.

Just as he had been seduced by the potential for victory in the Ardennes, Hitler now pinned all his hopes on Hungary, which he hoped could quench Germany's desperate thirst for oil. Particulary tempting were those around Hungary's Lake Balaton, in addition to the wells of Zisterdorf in Austria. The portents, though, were not good. The start of December 1944 had seen the Red Army occupy eastern Hungary. It had succeeded in crossing the Danube to the West and subsequently establishing a large bridgehead. The Germans had been obliged to pull back to a line southwest of Budapest on Lake Valence and Lake Balaton. In the closing weeks of 1944, two Soviet army groups, the 2nd and 3rd Ukrainian Fronts, unleashed a major offensive to encircle Budapest and crush all opposition.

Mounting a stout but ultimately doomed defence was *SS-Obergruppenführer* Karl Pfeffer von Wildenbruch's 9th *Gebirgskorps* (mountain corps), which included two cavalry divisions, the severely weakened Panzergrenadier division *Feldherrnhalle,* and units of the German and Hungarian armies and

Left: A surprisingly cheerful photograph shows *Waffen-SS* troops relaxing before their next attack in Hungary in early 1945. The standing panzergrenadier carries a *Panzerfaust* over his shoulder.

police. The total strength was reckoned at between 40,000 and 70,000 men. The IV SS Panzer Corps, under *Obergruppenführer* Herbert Gille, consisting of the 3rd SS Panzer Division *Totenkopf* and 5th SS Panzer Division *Wiking,* and buttressed by forces mustered from Galicia, attacked on the night of 1 January 1945.

SURPRISE ATTACK

Hubert Meyer, in his history of the *Hitlerjugend* Division, wrote that the attack surprised the Soviets: 'They had not thought it possible that the German leadership would be able to mount a counterattack with appreciable forces.' The Germans pushed through the Vertes mountains to within 21km (13 miles) of Budapest. Though the Soviets lost little time in recovering their defensive line, Gille was confident of attaining a breakthrough to Budapest. But Army Group South, acknowledging other plans by Hitler and the *Oberkommando der Wehrmacht* (OKW, the German High Command), called a halt. An eyewitness stated:

'The head of our assault could see the panorama of the city in their binoculars. We were disappointed and we could not believe the attack was stopped. Our morale was excellent and we knew we could free our comrades next day.'

Hitler favoured a fresh plan of attack – to destroy all Soviet troops north of a line drawn from Lake Balaton through Szekesfeherfvar to Budapest, and then to take the city. At first this seemed successful, but it exhausted the attacking force. This weakness was sensed by Marshal Rodion Malinovsky, the veteran of Stalingrad, who then went over to the attack. The Germans were unable to withstand the force of the Soviet onslaught.

BREAKOUT ATTEMPT

On 11 February 1945, the defenders inside Budapest, bereft of ammunition, made a last desperate bid to break out on their own. The result was as futile as it was tragic. The Soviet assault began with rockets aimed at the buildings in Buda. Many who had taken refuge there emerged, armed solely with machine pistols. They met a withering wall of fire, and scores were cut down within minutes. Those who survived rockets and artillery then had to contend with masses of Soviet infantry. A bare 780 reached the German lines two days later, while the majority of Germans and Hungarians were killed. The Soviets searched the rubble for survivors, butchering Germans where they lay exhausted or wounded. Trucks with loudspeakers drove up to the woods of the Buda hills, broadcasting appeals to those in hiding to come out, promising that they would be 'treated decently'. Those that did emerge were shot down, while the Hungarians were given the choice of internment or joining the Soviets. The Buda side of the city fell on 14 February. Over 51 days, the Germans had lost more than 70,000 men. And by now, the Soviets were over the Oder and Berlin was a mere 70km (43 miles) away.

Hitler's next plan, *Frühlingserwachen* (Operation Spring Awakening), was to be launched in western Hungary on 6 March. If successful, it would clear all Soviet forces west of the Danube and north of the Drva river to secure the vital oil deposits. In the

Right: Secure in his wood-lined bunker, a *Hitlerjugend* panzergrenadier readies his *Panzerfaust* for the next Soviet attack. Resting against the bunker roof is a rifle grenade launcher.

meantime, General Otto Wohler's Army Group South lay in a great arc west of the Danube, its boundaries extending from the Drau to the western edge of Lake Balaton.

At Lake Balaton, the line swung westwards to the Vertes mountains and then to the substantial bridgehead established by the Soviets on the northern bank of the Danube at Gran. This bridgehead was of crucial importance to the Germans, who saw it as a likely assembly area from where the Soviets would thrust towards Vienna. It therefore had to be eliminated before the start of Spring Awakening.

The Gran operation received the codename *Sud Wind* (South Wind). On 13 February, the commander of German Eighth Army issued the instruction:

'To attack, concentrating all available infantry and armoured forces, and accepting the consequent weakening of other front sectors, with the newly arrived I SS Panzer Corps... After a short artillery bombardment, to thrust from the north, to destroy the enemy in the Gran bridgehead.'

During the assault, *Hitlerjugend* fell in behind the *Leibstandarte* with 26th SS Panzer Grenadier Regiment committed to the right flank of its fellow division to secure the crossing of the Partizs canal. The 1st Battalion under the command of *SS-Sturmbannführer* Kostenbader crossed to the north of Gbelce village. The 2nd Battalion followed it into the shallow bridgehead and consolidated the position, managing to secure a small canal crossing that could take wheeled vehicles. During the night, the Russians attacked, striking with an infantry battalion and at least two T-34/85s. They were beaten off, but the casualties proved heavy. A rush was then made to plug any gap to the south of the canal where the Soviets were likely to penetrate, and this was achieved without opposition.

Hitler's insistence on undertaking Spring Awakening provoked severe opposition, notably from

Right: In the early stage of Operation Spring Awakening, the morale of the Sixth SS Panzer Army was high. These panzergrenadiers seem grimly determined, passing the bodies of Soviet soldiers.

Hans Guderian, as acting Chief of Staff, who argued that it was vital for the threat to the Eastern front to be countered. He had already spent time pleading with Hitler for the release of troops from the Ardennes and from the Upper Rhine for that purpose. Guderian suggested that Sixth SS Panzer Army should be brought to bear in the battle for the Oder, where two army groups were facing destruction by the Red Army. To Hitler, his description of Hungary as a secondary theatre had been as a red rag to a bull. The Führer had raved, 'I'm going to attack the Russians where they least expect it! The Sixth Panzer Army is off to Budapest! If we start an offensive in Hungary, the Russians will have to go too.' Guderian had a temper to match Hitler's, but all arguments had proved in vain, not least Guderian's point that shunting an entire army across Europe along poor rail communications, rather than straight to Berlin, must keep it out of action and useless for months.

In preparation for Spring Awakening, elaborate security plans were drawn up. The men of Sixth SS Panzer Army were ordered to remove their sleeve bands before the move from the area of Cologne began. To allay Allied suspicions that a major move was underway, the various groups taking part in the fighting were given a cover identity that downgraded their true status. Thus Sepp Dietrich, as Commander of Sixth SS Panzer Army, received the title *Hoherer Pionierführer Ungarn* (Senior Commander, Engineers Hungary), while 12th SS Panzer Division *Hitlerjugend* was designated *Ersatzstaffel Wiking* (Viking Replacement Squadron). 1st SS Panzer Division *Leibstandarte Adolf Hitler* was cloaked as *Ersatzstaffel Totenkopf* (Death's Head Replacement Squadron) and its regiments were described as *Baustabe* (construction staff). The 2nd SS Panzer Division *Das Reich* became *Ausbildungsgruppe Nord* (Training Group North).

Any suggestion that the various units, whatever their designation, could be refitted in advance – a matter of routine under normal circumstances – was out of the question. Replacements of personnel and material reached the trains at the time they were being loaded for departure. When the divisions left the Rhineland, they faced unpredictable connections and a constant shortage of fuel. Weather conditions

were atrocious. Heavy snow in late February was followed by a sudden rise in temperature at the turn of the month. Tanks could not move under the cover of night, and when they did try, they became stuck and were unable to be released until morning light. The month of March brought blizzard conditions, and the tanks could not move at all.

ARMY GROUP SOUTH

With its arrival, the Sixth SS Panzer Army was once more on the strength of Army Group South. It took part in the lightning assault that secured the Gran bridgehead on 17 February. Losses were put at more than 1000 panzergrenadiers from each of the SS divisions – and that before the start of Spring Awakening on 6 March. Two days later, the weather showed scant improvement, temperatures remaining below freezing. Reconnaissance revealed a pull-out by the Soviets from the area around Budapest and their bridgehead at the Drau river, in preparation for an attack against the German defences. In anticipation of this, German army units intent on closing with the Red Army had raced in a fast motor-boat assault across the Drau; the Bulgarian defenders, by now unwilling Russian allies, were effectively broken. From Sixth SS Panzer Army came the main thrust; the *Hitlerjugend* and *Leibstandarte* divisions forced the canal bridgehead.

It was an achievement made despite unspeakable conditions. The first shock came with the order to start the engines of the panzers; at first, this proved impossible, since water had seeped into the fuel tanks. Mechanics, obliged to operate amid a cascade of shelling, went about the frustrating and time-wasting task of draining out the contaminated fuel, and there was a desperate search for fresh supplies.

Initially, the morale of the forces of the *Hitlerjugend*, in common with the rest of Dietrich's manpower, was excellent, since at last this was a battle that had clear-cut objectives. The mood of

Right: Two *Waffen-SS* guards in Hungary well equipped for the cold with sheepskin coats over their greatcoats. As the war neared its end, many soldiers equipped themselves as best they could.

Above: *Hitlerjugend* men move quickly to counteract a Soviet tank attack. The man in front carries a *Panzerschreck*, a German copy of the American bazooka, while his companion holds a *Panzerfaust*.

Right: A map showing Sixth SS Panzer Army's thrust towards Budapest, and the subsequent Soviet movements towards Vienna and the heart of the Third Reich. The Austrian capital did not resist the Red Army for long.

optimism did not last long. At its very first objective, the division ran into trouble around the village of Puszta. In common with most others, this had been heavily fortified. The Soviets turned their full strength on the men of *Hitlerjugend*'s 26th Panzer Grenadier Regiment, which was all but annihilated. It was some consolation that the village of Igar was secured by the *Hitlerjugend*. Enemy positions were particularly strong around the village and farming area of Deg, and it was here that the division received a further major blow to morale. During an attack by Soviet combat aircraft, *Sturmbannführer* Kostgenbader, the commander of 26th Panzer Grenadier

Regiment – described by Hubert Meyer as 'an outstanding and brave leader' – was killed.

An important obstacle to the attack on Deg was a road junction situated to the east of Pinkocz-Puszta. *Haupsturmführer* Hans Siegel was despatched with two formidably armoured companies to eliminate this before the attack on Deg itself, which was planned for the morning of 8 March. The Germans shelled a knot of dug-in anti tank guns. Hubert Meyer quotes from Siegel's report:

'The concentrated force of fire and movement, added to which was the din of motors and the rattle of the tracked vehicles firing tracers in front of them, explosions from mortar shells hurled from armoured personnel carriers on the move, all that happening during otherwise total darkness, discouraging probably even the most hardened Red Army man....We overran the anti-tank barrier and the fortified positions without losses... Through the dawn, we arrived unscathed in Deg.'

The dawn haze was a useful cloak for the attack on Deg around which extensive minefields had been cleared. Pursuit of a withdrawing Soviet column was frustrated by a panzer company bogged down in marshy terrain and it was evening before it was mobile again. Outside Deg village, a single panzer, whose gunner had just homed in on his target, came under fire, and although it did not explode, was disabled. The rest of the panzers were inside the village

and out of sight. Siegel, feeling cut off, seized on a messenger with a motorcycle and leapt onto the back, perched on its carrier, roaring into the village. The panzers, as it turned out, arrived safely. There had been an encounter with around a dozen 10cm (3.9in) Russian assault guns, whose crews had been taken by surprise. Some managed to escape, and those who were able made their getaway from the opposite end of the village to the south and south east. Ahead of the panzer flak group, a Russian assault gun had been readied, its barrel facing forward. A panzer hammered a round into its rear and the assault gun blew up and burned out.

Elsewhere, there was bitter fighting at Simontornya and Azora, two towns to the east of the Sio Canal and Lake Balaton. The SS forces had to hold these before

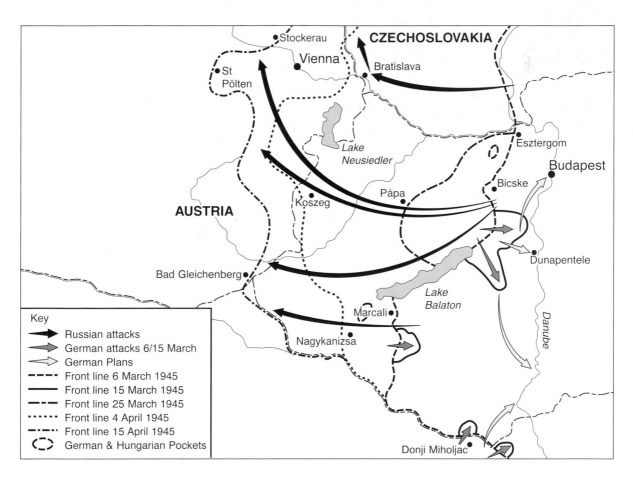

141

Above: Waiting for the enemy. A *Hitlerjugend* panzer-grenadier pauses from observing the Soviet lines with his binoculars. Note his Kar 98K rifle ready for action, and a stick grenade in the foreground within easy reach.

Right: A patrol returns to the German front line in Hungary, watched by a machine gunner from his protected position. By this point, the Soviet advance was most delayed by the need to wait for fresh supplies.

their forces could swing the direction of their advance southwards. Aware of the German need to secure these positions, the Soviets fought tenaciously. By 9 March, II SS Panzer Corps, with the *Leibstandarte* Division in the van, had broken through the CXXXV Red Infantry Corps. The soldiers, however, were exhausted and the drive began to falter, the momentum to slacken. To prevent inevitable disaster, Sepp Dietrich sped to these advanced positions to spur on the panzergrenadiers. The men of *Leibstandarte* were indeed inspired by the presence of their former commander, and pushed ahead. But II SS Panzer Corps was unable to maintain their pace. This slowed the assault, although progress continued to be made. The last gasps of resistance were stifled by the 2nd Panzer Grenadier Regiment of

the *Leibstandarte*, which advanced to the cemetery in Simontornya, on the town's southern edge.

Best Efforts

Hitlerjugend's 3rd Pioneer Company, along with its sister company from the *Leibstandarte*, redoubled their efforts to bridge the Sio. This was an operation that could be undertaken only at night, out of sight of Russian artillery fire. But there was no chance to secure the bridge or establish another bridgehead beyond it. The hill south of the canal had been turned into a strong defensive position by the Soviets, with their seemingly limitless resources of manpower.

In the *Hitlerjugend*, life was notably uncomfortable for tank crews. As recorded by Hubert Meyer,

Above: *Waffen-SS* panzergrenadiers form a hasty defence line in Hungary in 1945. Food, fuel and ammunition was in short supply, but the German defenders made the Red Army fight hard for every piece of ground gained.

Right: Panzergrenadiers of the Sixth SS Panzer Army huddle in their trench, fearful of an air attack by Soviet fighter-bombers. Only the most fanatical of Nazis now believed that the war could still be won.

Oberscharführer Willy Kretschmar, of 5th Panzer Company, later recalled:

'The Pioneers had just cleared the first mines when there were 10 to 15 flashes from the rising terrain behind the Sio Canal. That made it clear to me that we were facing a strong anti-tank position. I was just about to indicate the target to the gunner when there were two or three bangs on the Panzer. I shouted to the driver, "Back up – let's go!" He replied, "I can't, the gas pedal is ripped out. The sun is shining in here." I gave orders to bail out. Except for the radio operator, we all got out and assembled behind the Panzer. Finally, the radio operator's hatch opened

and Stefan came out white as chalk. Because of the hit to the transmission, he had probably inhaled fumes from the oil.'

DASH FOR COVER

The men sprinted for cover behind another panzer. Meanwhile, the Soviet infantry which had emerged from its trenches, in an attempt to kill or capture the crew, was pinned down by explosive shells and machine-gun fire. Armoured personnel carriers, which had originally pulled back during the attack, were at last able to move forward again, taking Kretschmar's crew and two others back to their

Left: In the retreat to Austria, essential supplies – and even basic comforts like cigarettes – were running low. Here a tank crew member shares a cigarette with a comrade from Sixth SS Panzer Army.

Above: Panthers from the Sixth SS Panzer Army in Hungary in 1945. The lack of fuel and overwhelming numbers opposing them meant that there was no chance of a return to a *Blitzkrieg*-style war for these tanks.

starting position. The body of a killed company squad leader was placed in an engine compartment, and the carriers were able to reach safety, thanks to cover provided by a Panther tank, which was later knocked out.

To add to the Germans' difficulties, the bridge sustained constant damage from artillery fire and partly collapsed under the weight of a panzer. As a result of the Soviet fire, vehicles tended to bunch too close together in an attempt to minimize their exposure, thus adding to the congestion and weight on the bridge.

Safe in Berlin, Josef Goebbels commented:

'I have the impression that our offensive has bogged down. Admittedly, Sepp Dietrich has succeeded in forming a bridgehead across the Sio, but it is questionable whether he can advance out of it.'

In the circumstances, Goebbels's pessimism could perhaps have been excused. Nevertheless, on 11 March, Simontornya was captured, but not without tough resistance, which necessitated bloody house-to-house combat. The day after the bridgehead over the Sio Canal was established, fighting reached a new peak of ferocity as both sides struggled for the initiative.

Left: A rearguard from the *Hitlerjugend* at the side of a road out of an Hungarian village watch the stream of traffic, led by a half track towing a field piece, heading back towards Germany in the spring of 1945.

Meanwhile, the presence of Dietrich's units in Hungary had deprived the German defensive line on the Oder river of badly needed strength. Since early February the Germans had erected formidable defences around the capital. A solid toehold was kept by the Germans on the east bank of the Oder river at Kostrzyn (at the time known as Kustrin) which was astride the direct route west to Berlin. However bridgeheads had been seized by the Russians over the river's southern part, notwithstanding desperate resistance from the units of Army Group Centre. By the end of the month, Soviet forces had, from the junction of the Oder and Neisse rivers, reached a position just 105km (65 miles) south east of Berlin.

Ahead lay other disasters for the Germans in Silesia in southern Poland. Army Group South in Hungary faced outflanking in the north with Malinkovsky's 2nd Ukrainian Front thrusting towards Bratislava on the Danube in southern Czechoslovakia. Meanwhile Tolbukhin's 3rd Ukrainian Front was pushing Wohler's Army Group South back towards Austria.

RETREAT

From now on, breakthroughs by the Germans were rare. After 18 March, barely 11 days after the commencement of Spring Awakening, the Soviet advance became unstoppable. The Soviets made deep penetrations west of the Vertes mountains and were fast approaching Lake Balaton. The German defence was successful at the town of Balinka, but the Soviets redressed the balance by securing Isztmir. In fact, no matter the location, German gains were now puny and shortlived. The main problem for the Germans was the lack of supplies for the forward positions, petrol and ammunition in particular was in short supply.

The closing days of the month saw the Sixth SS Panzer Army withdrawing westward in its frantic bid to hold 150km (93 miles) of front between the Danube and Lake Balaton. It had only six battalions.

There was no longer a front of any substance, only isolated strongpoints. To the north of the Raab river lay Odenburg, on the direct route to Vienna. On 1 April 1945, the Germans tried to block enemy forces at this point, but the Soviets swept past in an outflanking move. The only German defence came from tank trains. Formed to conserve fuel, these involved one or two machines towing a number of others, thus enabling sufficient tanks to be saved to reform some of the shattered companies.

The German cause was hopeless, but the *Hitlerjugend* made some spirited final attacks. In the Sixth SS Panzer Army sector, the *Das Reich* and 6th Panzer Divisions managed to break free from the area to the south of Lake Valencei, and crossed the path of the advancing Red Army, with the aim of plugging the Soviet breakthrough in the Vertes Hills. For the 1st SS Panzer Division, the only action was withdrawal. Nonetheless, it was able to stem a powerful Red Army force, which was attacking between the lake and the area of Szekesfehervar. It also linked up with units of 5th SS Panzer Division *Wiking*, which was still managing to hold on to parts of the town.

WITHDRAWAL

The withdrawal of the Sixth SS Panzer Army to the Raab could no longer be delayed. It was a chaotic, perilous process, and scores of vehicles were bogged down in mud. Much heavy equipment had to be either abandoned or destroyed. The weather was so bad that even the Soviets were delayed by it. Indeed, General (later Marshal) Fedor I Malinovsky, the 56-year-old Soviet Commander and captor of Budapest, whose Fifty-Seventh Army had played a key role in the encirclement of the Germans at Stalingrad, now had Stalin breathing down his neck, furious at the slowness of the advance. The order went out to the Soviet Sixth Tank Army that, regardless of loss in manpower,

Right: Within Germany itself, defence had become the province of the *Volksturm*, an ill-equipped and ill-trained mix of Hitler Youth members, old men and disabled veterans soon to be pitted against the Red Army's tanks.

the pace must be forced. The result was success, but at the cost of 267 Red Army tanks.

By the beginning of April, the much-vaunted German Tiger II tanks were mere battered hulks and the Hungarian Third Army, which had been covering Dietrich's left flank, was blown to oblivion. The Soviet 3rd Ukrainian Front sealed off the city on three sides,

joining hands with Marshal Rodion Malinovsky's 2nd Ukrainian Front, whose Forty-Sixth Army sped down from the northeast towards the Austrian capital, Vienna. The *Hitlerjugend*, which by now had long been a division in name only, was left to fight its way through Odenburg and its occupying Soviet forces, who inflicted heavy casualties. But even at this late

Above: By the time the remnants of the *Hitlerjugend* Division reached Austria, they were a pale imitation of themselves only a year before. Hard fighting had seen their numbers decline dramatically.

stage, the division was able to avoid encirclement. Thus the sweepings of *Hitlerjugend* somehow man-

aged to make for the north of Odenburg in the direction of Wiener Neustadt and the roads to Vienna.

SS-Oberführer Hugo Kraas reported:

'*Kampfgruppe* 26 and the Divisional staff hung on with their last remaining strength. In the afternoon, another attack, breakthrough and counterattack.'

A welcome, but disappointingly brief, respite was recorded by one *Kampfgruppe*. On the day before Easter Sunday, it overcame resistance in a village beyond the Weiner Neustadt area. Soviet cartridges that fitted carbines and assault rifles were eagerly seized. The grateful villagers brought the men hot coffee, sandwiches and Easter eggs. But then the men learnt that the Soviets were in sight of Vienna, and the order came to abandon the village.

As for Sepp Dietrich, he considered that his task – possibly his only remaining task – was to use his army to hold the line, covering the flank of the German armies in Czechoslovakia, where the Soviets for the moment were concentrating. It was wishful thinking. The mass of 1st SS Panzer Division *Leibstandarte* was burnt out. As for 12th SS Panzer Division *Hitlerjugend*, it was severely weakened, and the other divisions in the army were either of average strength or were shadows of their former selves.

Hitler now gave Sepp Dietrich and Sixth SS Panzer Army a new, well-nigh impossible task – to defend Vienna from the Red Army. The Führer's veteran gladiator, who had several times requested in vain for the offensive in Hungary to be broken off, was under no illusions. With some exaggeration and rueful humour he remarked: 'We call ourselves Sixth SS Panzer Army because we have only six tanks left.' Indeed, matters were so bad that he was obliged to thrust pupils of the Babenbergerburg military academy into the front line. His ranks were further swelled by low-calibre recruits: *Luftwaffe* pilots bereft of aircraft to fly, sweepings of *Kreigsmarine* from ships never destined to sail, and factory workers. Quaking with terror under fire, these men became dangerous distractions to the battle-hardened SS men.

By 10 April, the Soviets were in the centre of Vienna, which was virtually encircled by the Red Army. The decision to evacuate the city was not a matter for Sepp Dietrich, but rather Hitler himself. Finally, the Führer ordered the withdrawal across the Danube. Dietrich's last order was given to Baldur von Schirach, who had remained in Vienna as *Gauleiter* but who, in a reverse that severely pricked his vanity, had been ordered to serve as Dietrich's liaison officer. The orders given to the one-time *Reichsjugendführer* were to drive to the Tyrol and check on reception centres for the army, refugees and wounded.

SANCTUARY

For the men of the *Hitlerjugend,* the main objective now that the war was rapidly coming to a conclusion, was to reach the sanctuary of the American lines to surrender. Many made for those of the US 65th Division, which was located near the Enns river. Late in the afternoon, tired, bedraggled lines of the division's soldiers made to cross a bridge. A previously erected barricade had only been partly cleared, which meant that there was room for just a single truck to cross at a time. Suddenly, panic broke out as someone yelled 'Rusky'. What had been an orderly line became a surging, thrusting mass. Men were crushed to death in the stampede while others, unable to reach the bridge because of the crowd, abandoned the attempt and fanned out along the river back, still shouting. 'Rusky, Rusky'. The approach of a Red Army medium tank increased the panic. From its turret, a lieutenant laughed as an estimated 6000 men scrambled frantically to escape his single gun.

It was on the banks of the Enns that the surrender of the division was accepted by the Americans. Some had worried that the Soviets, whom *Hitlerjugend* had most recently been fighting, would insist that any surrender be made to them.

Hubert Meyer and an orderly officer were taken by jeep to what appeared to be a commandeered factory, where a sentry stood on guard. The two men were ushered into a room whose only furniture was a large table, covered with maps. Meyer was asked to indicate where the division was located and how many men had survived. He hazarded a figure of 10,000 survivors, an answer that was received with delight. Meyer noticed the presence of bottles and

glasses, which suggested that the Americans had already been celebrating.

The American staff officer next announced the conditions for surrender. Hostilities were to cease by midnight on 8 May, by which time all troops had to be across the demarcation line of the Enns river, between the American and Soviet lines; any delay would result in the Soviets taking the division prisoner. All weapons were to be unloaded 2km (1 mile) from the river and small arms removed. Tanks and guns were to follow behind on trucks, with the tanks pointing their guns in the air. Vehicles were required to fly white flags.

On this last point, Hugo Kraas was later to prove obdurate, ordering that no white flags be flown. He thanked each member of the division for their value and loyalty, and urged that, in memory of their dead comrades, the men maintain a spirit of camaraderie during the rebuilding of the Fatherland. He concluded:

'We set out on the bitterest journey of our life as soldiers with our heads held high. In quiet composure, we will march towards our destiny. We have fought bravely and with integrity in all theatres of war. Still, the war is lost. Long live Germany.'

On the morning of the deadline, Kraas and Meyer drove to Enns, stopping only to bury their weapons in a gravel pit. The surrendering troops marched past, mounted as if on parade, with perfect bearing.

At this point, there was a dramatic incident. A knot of *Wehrmacht* vehicles appeared, carrying former prisoners from the nearby Mauthausen concentration camp, their weapons at the ready. As they drove along the *Hitlerjugend* column, they began looting its vehicles. In his book *Men of Steel: I SS Panzer Corps 1944–45 — The Ardennes and Eastern Front,* Michael Reynolds guesses that this was a deliberate piece of stage management designed by the Americans to humiliate the surrendering Germans. If this were so, Reynolds points out, the *Hitlerjugend* could count

Right: A line-up of Hitler Youth were afforded their last glimpse of the Führer in the Berlin Chancellery garden on 20 April 1945, his 56th birthday. The youngest of these boy defenders of the capital was 12 years old.

itself fortunate. Only nine days before, American troops had been so enraged at the atrocities they found when they liberated Dachau that they summarily executed 21 guards, including 17 SS men.

These were the last hours of the 12th SS Panzer Division *Hitlerjugend*. In 1944, its strength had been put at 21,300. Now just 455 had survived to go into captivity. The only weapons remaining were 16 tanks, 21 howitzers, assorted rocket launchers and captured Soviet 76.2cm (3in) guns.

Nonetheless, the *Hitlerjugend* had made a decisive contribution to the destruction of the Gran bridgehead and the breasting of the Sio canal near Simontornya during the Lake Balaton offensive. The hope of a lasting defence against the enemy had been dashed, but that was scarcely the fault of the men of *Hitlerjugend*. As Meyer put it:

'They were predominantly soldiers who had hardly been provided with infantry training and had never been part of a fighting force... They were thrown abruptly into the whirlpool of bloody rearguard fighting which demanded the utmost physical and mental resistance. That had to reach beyond their strength.'

Not the least of their reasons for fighting so fanatically was the knowledge that if they were captured by the Soviets, their certain fate was a painful death.

But it has to be said of the *Hitlerjugend* that their fanaticism and individual brutality diluted any sympathy felt for them. One striking example, which happened during the fighting around Caen, can serve. Two British infantrymen encountered a seriously wounded member of the division. They tried to render medical aid and also gave him water. While his head was being bandaged, he reached slowly for his camouflage smock, and managed to snatch a Walther pistol. Only the fact that he was seriously injured saved the life of his benefactors. The two British soldiers seized the gun and left the young German to die.

In his book *Hitler's Children: The Hitler Youth and SS*, the author Gerhard Rempel firmly points the finger of blame for the brainwashing of Germany's youth, declaring: 'The separate growth of the *Hitlerjugend* and SS as organizations depended on the active collaboration of the elite who controlled them.' It is they, the Nazi leadership, who were ultimately responsible for the corruption of an entire generation, the scars of which are only now finally healing over.

CHAPTER EIGHT

KEY FIGURES

From German-American playboys like Baldur von Schirach to hard-bitten warriors like Kurt Meyer, a number of individuals played an important part in shaping the *Hitlerjugend* Division. Some, like Fritz Witt, had previously had a successful career elsewhere in the *Waffen-SS*.

BALDUR VON SCHIRACH

Baldur von Schirach was born in Berlin on March 9 1907, the first of four children of a well-to-do-family. Although three-quarters American, he joined the Young German League at the age of 10 and became fully absorbed in the usual round of camp fires, hikes and singing sessions. His interest in radical politics was fuelled by the grim realities of life in the Weimar Republic after World War I. His father, Carl Bailey-Norris von Schirach, a former officer in the Kaiser's army, lost his job as a theatre director, along with much of the family money.

Like so many of his generation at this time, the young Baldur became absorbed by the preoccupations of a rootless upper and middle class – namely the belief that the Treaty of Versailles was unjust, and, above all, that it was the Jews who were responsible for all social and economic ills. Von Schirach eagerly embraced the fanatical racism expounded in such books as Houston Stewart Chamberlain's *The Foundations of the 19th Century* and Henry Ford's *The International Jew*. From this, it was but a step to absorb-

Left: A trumpeter of the *Hitler Jugend* during a Nazi rally before the war. Baldur von Schirach played an important part in establishing the ceremonial traditions of the Hitler Youth, and such pageantry stimulated recruitment.

ing the ranting of the anti-Jewish, anti-Communist fanatic Alfred Rosenberg, the 'philosopher' of the Nazi party and one of the strongest intellectual influences on Adolf Hitler.

For Hitler, whose *Mein Kampf* also shaped von Schirach's views, their first meeting in Weimar 1926 proved heaven-sent; the Nazi leader was keen to refine the image of the party, whose most high-profile exponents were the brash street-brawlers of the *Sturm Abteilung* (SA, storm troopers). Smooth and voluble, von Schirach seemed the ideal acolyte. From the very start, Hitler saw the young man not simply as a party member, but as a man who could fulfil a specific need – the recruitment of contemporaries for the Nazi movement.

At Munich, the cradle of National Socialism, von Schirach was put to work, enrolling at the university as a member of the SA with the specific task of attracting fellow students. By 1929, he had become chief of the university's National Socialist Students' Union. It was here that a fellow student, Henrietta Hoffmann, first met him. Both worked on producing Nazi propaganda leaflets and an underground newspaper.

In her memoirs, Henrietta recalled:

'One day a young man in a light suit came running up the stairs whistling *Yankee Doodle Dandy*. He was the leader of the students' association, chief publisher and editor – Baldur von Schirach, who had just returned from a trip to America. Baldur was 23 years old. The female members, including myself, worked in an honorary capacity… One of my jobs was to address the wrappers of the little news sheet. Month after month, we issued leaflets, distributing them on the steps of the university.'

Heinrich Hoffmann, the famous photographer and friend of Hitler, was Henrietta's father, a fact that was not lost on von Schirach. The couple later married.

Von Schirach worked his passage industriously, careful to extol his Führer and National Socialism at every conceivable opportunity, including writing flowery verse about 'this genius grazing the stars' and 'everything is the love of Adolf Hitler.' His reward was promotion to *Jugendführer des Deutschen Reiches*, a post originally under the control of the Ministry of the Interior and its leader Wilhelm Frick. After December 1 1936, it rated an office in the Reich Cabinet. At 29, von Schirach thus became a key figure in the Third Reich, and had the advantage of reporting directly to Hitler.

Inevitably, this brought him detractors and enemies, who spoke of the man's oily and effeminate manner. There were rumours of a white bedroom, decked out with delicate lace curtains, and whispers of homosexuality, which was hardly surprising since von Schirach had served in the SA where it was rampant.

Indeed, Airey Neave, a future British Member of Parliament, who in 1946 served the indictments on the defendants at Nuremberg at the International Military Tribunal, later describes von Schirach as having an appearance that was 'bisexual and soft with *thé-dansant* eyes. He looked a man who might be dangerous to small boys… He was wet, self-deluded and arrogant.'

This, however, left out of account two elements of von Schirach's character: considerable organizational ability and more than a streak of ruthlessness. His new position gave him the power to supervise the entire youth of a Germany that was becoming progressively

Right: Baldur von Schirach (standing) as *Reichsjugendführer*, giving a morale boosting speech to an audience of *Hitler Jugend* and *Bund Deutscher Madel* (BDM – the League of German Girls).

more Nazified. The official policy of the *Hitler Jugend* was *Gleichstellung* – the coordination and integration of all other youth organizations, together with a total ban on those remaining outside it and thus deemed 'traitorous'. Offenders were tracked down by the full resources of the *SA*, the *SS* and its most potent arm, the *Gestapo,* and the *HJ Streifendienst*, the internal *Hitler Jugend* police.

There was an undertone of menace in the direct order issued by von Schirach:

Left: Seen here on a visit to Prague, Heinrich Himmler, as *Reichsführer-SS*, was not initially keen on the formation of a *Hitlerjugend* Division. On Himmler's immediate right stands Reinhard Heydrich.

as complaints necessitate further action, I shall initiate the necessary steps through the appropriate state institutions.'

One of the first targets was the dissident German Youth Movement and Eberhard Kobel, a prominent member. Along with his associates, Kobel was arrested and incarcerated in the cellars of the notorious Columbia-Haus in Berlin. He was later released, but only after being severely beaten up. In another more spectacular incident, von Schirach personally led a surprise raid with 50 of his followers on the offices of the National Central Committee (*Reichsausschuss*) of Youth Organisations. General Vogt, its head, was summarily dismissed, and its records confiscated. Von Schirach personally arranged a shotgun marriage, whereby the National Committee was absorbed into the *Hitler Jugend* and subsequently abolished.

Other organizations, even those known to be politically uncommitted, received the same treatment. Prominent among these was the Greater German Youth League, led by Admiral von Trotha, a veteran of the Kaiser's navy, of whom Von Schirach declared smoothly: 'This admirable and meritorious man adapted himself to the new situation by virtue of his soldierly sense of duty and his love for the younger generation.'

By December 1 1936, all German youth was organized from inside von Schirach's *Hitler Jugend*. At Reich Party Day in that same year, he was revelling in his success, while at the same time acknowledging with characteristic floridity the considerable debt owed to the Führer:

'One thing is stronger than you, my Führer. That is the love of young Germans for you. There are so many happy hours in the year of the youth. This, however, in every year is one of our happiest. Because more than any other people, my Führer, we feel ourselves to be chained to your person by your name. Your name is the happiness of the youth, your name, my Führer, is our immortality.'

'I hereby forbid any interference of the *Hitler Jugend* by other youth associations. If the behaviour of members of other youth associations gives cause for complaint, then the complaint is to be directed to me through the proper official channels. In so far

If von Schirach could be reasonably sure of the approval of Hitler, the same could not be said of other leading Nazis. Hermann Göring, no stranger to flamboyance himself, regarded the other man with open contempt. Others ridiculed his feverish attempts to curry favour by sporting Bavarian Lederhosen. But it was the streak of indulgence in his character that incensed many. At party rallies, *Hitler Jugend* leaders came to resent being put up in cheap hotels, while von Schirach himself chose an obviously deluxe establishment.

After his brief term of military service in the early months of World War II, von Schirach was approached by Hitler to become *Gauleiter* (district leader) of Vienna, while at the same time retaining all his party connections. He and his family moved to a lavishly appointed estate that had been sequestered from the Hapsburgs and required the attention of 17 servants.

The office of *Gauleiter* was but one of von Schirach's duties. He also held national office as a Reich Defence Commissioner, with responsibility for the *Gau* (provinces) of Vienna, Upper Danube and Lower Danube. This gave him an important role in planning the war economy, while the role of *Gauleiter* gave him responsibility for the administration of the municipal city of Vienna. This was far from being parish pump politics; all actions were subject to guidance and direct orders from Berlin, including the matter of the deportation of Jews – who numbered 150,000 in the Austrian capital alone. He urged Hans Frank, the Governor General of Occupied Poland, to take some 50,000 Jews from Vienna. The direct intervention of Hitler increased this figure to 60,000, and the deportations began early in the autumn of 1942.

Even if he had wished to do so, there was no way in which von Schirach could have retained his power if he had refused to implement the programme to deport Jews, and a general policy of forced and slave labour. This was the result of a decree of 6 April

Right: Attempts were made to affiliate the *Hitler Jugend* with nationalist youth movements outside Germany, including Spain's *Falange Espanola Tradiscionalista*, a member of which is seen here at a Nazi rally.

1942, issued by Fritz Sauckel, the *Generalbevoll-mächtigter für Arbeitseinsatz* (Minister of Labour with Special Powers of Plenipotentiary General for the Allocation of Labour). 'Allocation' meant deportation, of course, for those intended for slave labour. Sauckel was later to boast, 'Of the 5 million foreign workers who have come to Germany, fewer than 200,000 have come voluntarily.'

By the summer of 1944, events took an even more sinister turn. Von Schirach was ordered to accept 12,000 Jews for essential war work in Vienna. This was accompanied by the rider that those unable to work were to be subject to 'special action' – murder at the hands of the notorious *SS Einsatzgruppen* (extermination squads). What was more, von Schirach was in regular receipt of the secret distribution list issued by the Reich Main Security Department on the activities of the *Einsatzgruppen* – an important factor in the evidence that was presented at his trial at Nuremberg, and in the resulting sentence of 20 years.

However assiduous he may have been in carrying out his duties, von Schirach still had his enemies, who were prepared to denigrate both him and his wife. One opportunity arose when Henrietta was accused of buying a pair of stockings worth 20 marks from a store owned by Jews. Later in 1943, in an act of considerable courage, she criticized Hitler to his face for the treatment of Jews she had encountered on a trip to Amsterdam. She was told not to be sentimental. But this was the beginning of the end for the couple.

With the collapse of Nazi Germany, von Schirach took advantage of the general chaos and melted into the Austrian Tyrol. Since he spoke faultless English, he was able to adopt the name Richard Falk. Sprouting a beard, he worked for a time as an interpreter for the occupying Americans, and also wrote a novel, *The Secrets of Myrna Loy*. But, in the face of intensified hunts for former Nazis, he took a bold gamble and gave himself up.

Right: Artur Axmann congratulates survivors from the Falaise pocket in 1944. He took great interest in the *Hitlerjugend* Division until the war's end. He had earlier lost his right arm in combat in the Soviet Union.

His fawning attempts to gain the sympathy of his captors alienated both them and his fellow defendants. In the book *Nuremberg*, his personal record of the trial, Airey Neave wrote of his early meetings with the former *Hitler Jugend* leader, who invariably wore a smart dove-grey suit '… as if dressed for the Kürfurstendamm on a summer morning in the 1930s. Only the

hat and cane were missing… I found him strangely repellent. His attempt to make each interview into a social occasion, his colloqual speech, poised manner and smooth demeanour riled me… His face and figure suggested a surfeit of cream buns.'

Once arrested, von Schirach was ordered by General Patton to send a message to the surviving youth of the former Nazi Germany, telling them that there should be no underground movement, no myth to perpetuate the memory of Adolf Hitler and no anti-Semitism. At his trial, von Schirach confessed to the court that:

'It is my guilt that I educated youth for a man who committed a millionfold murders. I carry the guilt for

youth reared in an anti-Semitic state under anti-Semitic laws.'

Life in the jail at Nuremberg was grim. In her memoirs, *The Price of Glory*, Henrietta wrote:

'He and the other prisoners were shaved with a safety razor – no knives lest any of them tried to wrest one from the barber, which greatly amused him; almost in the same breath, however, he went on to describe the scene after the executions and the survivors standing naked and manacled in their cells, their hair cut short, each with a number. Later I found out – not from Baldur – that he and Speer had to clean the gymnasium in which the executions took place. From him not a word about the gallows and the view of the much-too-small, blood-smeared opening through which the corpses of the executed men disappeared.'

Von Schirach had fully expected the death sentence in the face of the indictment that accused him of authorizing, directing and 'participating in crimes against humanity... including particularly anti-Jewish measures.' In fact, he received 20 years, despite a doomed appeal to the judges from Henrietta that 'our children love America'.

The tribunal found him guilty on Count 4 – Crimes Against Humanity. The judgment read:

'Von Schirach used the *Hitler Jugend* to educate German youth "in the spirit of National Socialism" and subjected them to an extensive programme of Nazi propaganda... The Tribunal finds that von Schirach, while he did not originate the policy of deporting Jews from Vienna, participated in this deportation after he became *Gauleiter* of Vienna. He knew that the best that the Jews could hope for was a miserable existence in the Ghetto of the East. Bulletins describing the Jewish extermination were in his office.'

Even in Spandau jail in Berlin, von Schirach continued to irritate, maintaining an air of aloofness. In the book *Hitler's Elite*, Louis Snyder describes him striding '... around the compound in crumpled brown

Left: *Reichsjugendführer* **Artur Axmann speaking in Berlin at a meeting to boost German morale. As late as March 1945, Axmann was declaring: 'From the Hitler Youth has emerged a movement of young tank busters.'**

**Above: Axmann, who had served in combat with distinc-
tion before becoming *Reichsjugendführer*, was greatly
respected by his *Hitlerjugend* troops. Here he awards
medals to members of the division at Beverloo, Belgium.**

corduroy and wearing a dark-coloured nylon coat with
his monocle dangling from his neck outside it. He was
known for the neatness of his cell, where his favourite
Dunhill pipes were carefully stacked.'

He served his full term. His release in 1966 did not
mean a return to his wife; Henrietta had earlier
divorced him. He died at Krov on August 8 1974.

ARTUR AXMANN

The background and character of *Reichsjugendführer*
Artur Axmann could scarcely have been of greater con-
trast to that of his predecessor Baldur von Schirach,
described above. The choice of Axmann for the job
was almost certainly a deliberate move, intended to
counter the resentment felt by many important Nazi

figures at what had seen as von Schirach's arrogance
and self-indulgence.

Melita Maschmann, a member of the *Bund Deutscher
Madel* (BDM), the female equivalent of the *Hitler
Jugend* where she served as a press and propaganda
officer and worked closely with Axmann, described
him in her memoirs, *Account Rendered*:

'He came from so-called humble beginnings. He
was in a certain sense the proletarian showpiece of the
youth leadership corps: he was proof to us that every
German boy had a field marshal's baton in his knap-
sack. One was always hearing how he and his
brothers had been brought up by the widow of a factory worker, who had earned her living during the
depression by taking in washing. So far as I know, he
made his name in the Berlin Wedding district. At all
events, he started and ran units of the Hitler Youth
there amongst the young working-class boys.'

Throughout his career, Axmann enjoyed the considerable advantage of Himmler's respect and support.

This was due to his service on the Russian Front in 1941, when he sustained severe injuries and lost an arm. In Himmler's eyes, he had therefore become a war hero for the Fatherland, a distinction not shared by von Schirach.

What he did share with his predecessor, however, was an abundant energy. This had been revealed at an early age, when he formed the first *Hitler Jugend* group in Westphalia in 1928. Within five years he had been appointed chief of the Social Office of the Reich Youth Leadership. During this time, he had developed close ties with the rank and file SS, taking care to distance himself from their fierce rivals, the SA (Storm Troopers), who were to perish in the so-called 'Night of the Long Knives' in June 1934.

Himmler supported his appointment as *Reichs-jugendführer* at the age of 27, in place of von Schirach's former deputy, Hartmann Lauterbacher. The latter felt

some resentment at being passed over, and had to be content with the post of provincial leader in Hanover. Axmann's keen support for the formation of the *Hitlerjugend* Division, particularly in the light of Germany's worsening position on the eastern front, was not shared by Himmler at first. The *Reichsführer-SS* pinned his faith on the million or so men already under his command. Axmann privately dismissed many of these as being of dubious loyalty and fighting capabili-ty, but in public he held his tongue. He had to wait until the early spring of 1943 before the formation of the division was authorized, thus adding appreciably to his own power base and prestige.

Below: Observing exercises conducted by the newly formed *Hitlerjugend* Division in 1944 are, among others, Sepp Dietrich (crouching) and to the right of the picture, Artur Axmann and Fritz Witt, the division's commander.

On the home front, Axmann concentrated his energies on the privations suffered by Germans. By April 1942, basic regulations had been issued for 'the war service of the youth to ensure the feeding of the German people'. That summer, he introduced Operation Barefoot. *Hitler Jugend* members were told that leather and textiles were of critical importance when it came to equipping the fighting troops; youth was to 'play its part in conserving these important raw materials for our soldiers and to take care of their clothes and shoes.' Axmann instructed his followers to go around barefoot in the summer. It would be chic to 'wear things that are faded, worn out or patched.' He also ordered the sharpening up of the pre-military training of boys, to inculcate 'further

Below: Fritz Witt, who served with the *Leibstandarte* as a regimental commander, at Kharkov in March 1943. He was one of the select group of *Hitlerjugend* officers, NCOs and specialists drawn from the elite SS division.

orientation for their political and military duties'. For dissenters, punishments were severe and were handed out even for such activities as listening to British enemy broadcasts. On Axmann's recommendation, Himmler instructed Reinhard Heydrich, the head of the *Sicherheitsdienst* (SD, Security Service), to despatch these 'radio criminals' to concentration camps, where torture was commonplace.

Axmann remained tireless until the end, declaring 1944 as the 'Year of the Volunteer'. The best public speakers were despatched to promote enlistment in the *Wehrmacht* at ceremonial rallies. His care for the safety of his *Hitler Jugend* was apparent to Melita Maschmann, who accompanied him that year on a morale-boosting tour of West Germany:

'During one of these rallies the approach of enemy bomber formations was announced and it now emerged that the organizers of the meeting had not made the necessary provision for this eventuality. Axmann was so infuriated at the danger his young

audience had been subjected to by this oversight that he wanted to abandon his whole programme and go straight back to Berlin.'

The next year, amid the blackened ruins of the Reich's capital, *Hitler Jugend* amateurs and *Volkssturm* (People's Militia) received a message of defiance that showed Axmann had lost none of his fanaticism:

'The enemy stands in our homeland and is directly threatening our lives. Rather than let ourselves be annihilated or enslaved, we will fight hard and doggedly until the final victory.'

Within Berlin, General Karl Weidling's LVI Panzer Corps took the full brunt of the onslaught from the Red Army forces of General Georgi Zhukov. Though the men held out for a full 48 hours, causing heavy Soviet casualties, reinforcements promised from *SS Nordland* Division did not materialize and the arrival of 18th Panzer Grenadier Division was long delayed. Neither was there much help from Göring's 9th Parachute Division. Meanwhile, the Soviets carried out a classic horseshoe manoeuvre – hitting from both sides and encircling constantly. In consequence, Weidling was forced to change headquarters twice and take refuge in a cellar.

For Axmann, this presented an ideal opportunity. He ordered his *Hitler Jugend* to man the roads to the rear of LVI Panzer Corps. This proved too much for Weidling, who resolutely refused to have children sacrificed in a hopeless cause and ordered Axmann to rescind the order forthwith. The countermand, if indeed it was ever issued, did not reach the youngsters, who held the position. The Russians mowed them all down, save for two youths who had fallen asleep in a cellar during a lull in the battle.

The war effectively ended for Axmann in the Berlin *Führerbunker*, where he saw Hitler's body after his suicide. Axmann sought escape with, among others, Hitler's closest confidante, Martin Bormann, and the Führer's surgeon, Ludwig Stumpfegger. At 23:00 on May 1, the party, moving in small groups amid a cascade of Russian shells, made for the Friedrichstrasse station. The area was ablaze and the only progress was across the Spree river by an iron footbridge running parallel to the Weidendammer Bridge. Here, though, they encountered a solid anti-tank barrier and heavy Soviet fire.

Axmann tore off his uniform and threw away his medals. A Red Army outpost mistook him and his companions for *Volkssturm*. At the same time, German tanks appeared, affording the fugitives the break they needed. They were able to make their way as far as the Ziegelstrasse. Then a violent explosion struck the lead tank, stunning Bormann and Stumpfegger and wounding Axmann. For all three, there was no alternative but to retreat to the Weidendammer Bridge. From there, the men followed the tracks of the surface railway to the Lehrter station. It was here that Bormann and Stumpfegger elected to follow the Invalidenstrasse to the east while Axmann struck out to the west. But this route proved impossible and, faced with a Russian patrol, he retraced his steps. He later said that he then came across the corpses of Bormann and Stumpfegger, the moonlight shining on their faces. There were no signs of an explosion and Axmann assumed that both men had been shot in the back. He continued on his way, escaping from Berlin and spending the following six months on the run before he was captured.

The fate of Bormann and Stumpfegger could not be determined with any certainty; Axmann's statements were greeted with some suspicion, for he could have been harbouring his former comrades. Then, in December 1972, during construction near the Lehrter Station, two skeletons were unearthed and their identities determined conclusively after forensic examination.

Axmann escaped from Berlin to Mecklenburg in the Soviet Zone and was eventually arrested by the US Army Counter Intelligence Corps when he ventured into Upper Bavaria. During the interval, he had not been idle. In the winter of 1945–46, he and a partner organized the speedy transport of prominent Nazis to remote hiding places, all under the guise of legitimate transport businesses. These were wound up by Operation Nursery, an Allied intelligence initiative, which arrested around 1000 Germans suspected of involvement. Axmann was held until May 1946, when a de-Nazification court sentenced him to 39 months imprisonment, dating from his arrest. The court

Above: Fritz Witt (on left) moulded the 'Crack Babies' of the *Hitlerjugend* into a formidable fighting unit. He is shown here with one of his beloved cigars and 'Papa' Schuch of the *Leibstandarte* Division.

Right: At the age of 35, *SS-Standartenführer* Fritz Witt was appointed commander of the *Hitlerjugend* Division. Witt's service to Hitler dated back to March 1933; he was part of a guard formed to protect the Reich Chancellery.

apparently took into account signs that Axmann had showed remorse when faced with the accusation that he had sent out a battalion of about 600 boys of 15 and 16 as late as 23 April 1945 to defend the Pichelsdorf Bridge in Berlin.

His remorse, if genuine, proved somewhat selective. On release, he attached himself to a right-wing organization known as the Brotherhood, run by former members of the *Hitler Jugend,* the *Waffen-SS* and the former Nazi intelligence service. This in spite of the fact that he had been ordered to refrain from political activity and risked the forfeiture of his property.

On release, Artur Axmann worked as a salesman and died in Berlin on 24 October 1996. News of his death and burial were kept secret, reportedly to avoid any neo-Nazi demonstrations.

FRITZ WITT

Like so many of the leading figures in 12th SS Panzer Division *Hitlerjugend,* Fritz Witt joined from the elite *SS-Leibstandarte*, where he had built up an outstanding reputation. Born in 1908 at Hohenlimbourg in Westphalia, he joined the SS (as SS No 21518) and the Party (NSDAP No 816769) in 1931. Originally he had been a member of the tiny *Stabwache* (Staff Guard), whose members acted as Hitler's bodyguard during the Führer's public appearances. Within months of Hitler coming to power in January 1933, he had become an *SS-Untersturmführer,* having completed an infantry junior commanders' course. He took over a platoon in the 2nd Company of the *Leibstandarte* and was later seconded to become a company commander of the SS Regiment *Deutschland,* another formation of

the *SS-Verfügungstruppen,* which was eventually to form part of the *Waffen-SS.*

Shortly before World War II broke out, Witt was selected to serve with the Panzer Division *Kempf,* and during the Polish campaign of September 1939, he commanded a company. It was at this time that he gained a reputation for fearlessness under fire: during a patrol to the west of Modlin, he carried a wounded man on his back and brought him to safety. He was awarded both classes of the Iron Cross. The citation recorded that he was the first member of the *Kempf* Division to be so honoured and that this was a recognition of both his courage and the outstanding achievements of his company.

Other honours followed, including that of the Knight's Cross on 4 September 1940. With the rank of *Sturmbannführer,* Fritz Witt took over 1st Battalion of the *Leibstandarte* Division and led his men in the 1941 campaigns in Yugoslavia and Greece, spearheading the assault on the Klidi Pass, which was a significant contribution to the swift conclusion of the campaign in Greece. His service on the Eastern front and the battles along the Mius River brought him the German Cross in Gold, the Infantry Assault Badge, and, finally, the Oak Leaves.

With the *Leibstandarte*'s conversion to a panzer division in 1942, Witt took over 1st SS Panzer Grenadier Regiment, with the rank of *SS-Standartenführer.* In the following months, during intense winter engagements, he led one of the battle groups that succeeded in closing a gap in the German line at Merefa, south of Kharkov, and then eventually recapturing the city in March 1943. Blessed with considerable powers of organization and leadership, he was chosen, along with others from the *Leibstandarte,* to mould into a fighting unit the 'Crack Babies' of the 12th SS Division *Hitlerjugend.* Promoted to *SS-Brigadeführer und General-major der Waffen-SS* at the age of 35, Witt thus became the second youngest divisional commander in Germany's armed forces.

In the course of a pre-invasion reconnaissance in Normandy, Witt predicted that a large measure of Allied activity would be in the area of Carpiquet, which not only possessed an airfield but was excellent tank country. The 12th SS was favoured as the most effective force for a major counter attack. However, on D-Day in June 1944, the division was dispersed too widely to be wholly effective, even if it did manage to create a perimeter that was strong enough to frustrate the first bids of British Second Army to capture Caen.

Witt's insistence on being in the thick of the fighting earned him the respect of his colleagues, even though he lacked the buccaneering charisma of his successor Kurt 'Panzer' Meyer, and was regarded by some of his senior officers as over-impulsive. He was in the habit of visiting a unit of his command each day, and 14 June found him at divisional headquarters at Venoix. During the late morning, shells fell around the château. Witt, taking cover in a trench, was struck in the head by shrapnel and died of his wounds.

Fritz Witt was buried first in the château at Tillieres-sur-Avre, but was disinterred by the Allies and laid to rest eventually in the Germany military cemetery in Champigny St Andre, France. Upon hearing of the death of his former comrade, Sepp Dietrich exclaimed, 'That's one of the best gone. He was too good a soldier to stay alive for long.'

KURT MEYER

The fact that Kurt 'Panzer' Meyer was able to reach the rank of *Oberführer* and to become one of the most best known soldiers in Germany could be interpreted as a sharp slap in the face for the *Wehrmacht.* The latter had retained much of its class-conscious Prussian ethos, a legacy of pre-war days. Meyer, however, was born the son of a labourer, on 23 December 1910 in Jerxheim. Following an elementary education, he had worked as a miner. During a brief spell with the Mecklenburg Land Police, he was talent-spotted by the *Waffen-SS.* Once he had joined the *Leibstandarte,* promotion was rapid. By the outbreak of war, he had reached the rank of *SS-Hauptsturmführer.*

After action in Poland and France, he distinguished himself in Greece, storming the Klissura Pass. More than 600 prisoners were captured, including a regimental and three battalion commanders, at the cost to his own side of nine killed and 18 wounded. With the added muscle of a battle group based on the 3rd

Above: Kurt 'Panzer' Meyer (right), who was at one time the youngest SS divisional commander, is seen here (to his right) with Hubert Meyer, his immediate successor, and *SS-Sturmbannführer* Steineck (third from left).

Battalion, he then seized Kastoria, netting a further 1200 prisoners and 36 guns, resulting in total confusion among Greek forces. At the Corinth Canal, Meyer and a reconnaissance battalion seized a couple of fishing boats and captured the port of Patras, moving down the west coast of the Peloponnese.

During the advance on the Soviet Union in the summer of 1941, he spearheaded the *Leibstandarte* with such panache that, aided eagerly by the Nazi propaganda machine, he earned the additional nickname *der schnelle Meyer*. His exploits at Kharkov in 1943 brought him both additional notoriety and his Oak Leaves.

Apart from his talent as a soldier, Meyer inspired considerable loyalty among those who worked with him. This was strongly in evidence when he was transferred to command the newly formed 25th SS Panzer

Grenadier Regiment of the 12th SS Panzer Division *Hitlerjugend* as *SS-Standartenführer*. To counter the severe threat to Germany's fortunes of the 1944 Allied landings in Normandy, Meyer succeeded in moulding a woefully inexperienced bunch of former Hitler Youth into a fanatical fighting force, which put up stiff resistance against the Canadians at Caen. After the death of Fritz Witt, Meyer assumed control of the 12th SS Division on 16 June 1944. Within two weeks, he was promoted to *SS-Oberführer* and, at the age of 33, was the youngest of the senior officers and of the divisional commanders throughout the armed forces, securing his Swords to the Knight's Cross. By the time of his capture by the Allies on 6 September 1944, the division had been bled of 60 per cent of its men.

After the war, the *SS* was designated a criminal organization. Meyer was therefore investigated for possible prosecution as a member of the *Schützstaffel*. As a prisoner of the Allies, he was sent to England and held at the 'London Cage', the headquarters of the War Crimes Investigation Unit.

Left: 'Panzer' Meyer, here seen at the Battle of Kursk, had developed quite a reputation for himself by the time of his introduction to the *Hitlerjugend* as commander of its newly formed 25th SS Panzer Grenadier Regiment.

At around the same time that Meyer was being held, the Americans were interrogating 17-year-old former *SS-Stürmmann* Jan Jesionek. A conscript with the 15th Reconnaissance Company of the 25th SS Panzer Grenadier Regiment, he had been wounded at Bretteville on the night of 8/9 June 1944. After three months in hospital, he was sent to a replacement unit – and promptly deserted to the Americans.

During interrogation at Chartres, he claimed that on the morning of 8 June he had brought prisoners to the command post of the regiment at Abbaye Ardenne, located between Caen and Bretteville. Here he faced Kurt Meyer, who shouted at him: 'Why do you bring prisoners to the rear? The murderers do nothing but eat our rations.' Meyer then turned to another officer and declared, 'I don't want our prisoners brought here.'

Jesionek was then allowed to withdraw. On his way out, he spotted a pump in a courtyard and decided to take a quick wash. The prisoners he had brought in were then marched past, through what appeared to be an opening to a small park or garden. As they reached the opening, each was shot in the back of the head by an *SS-Unterscharführer.*

Jesionek's interrogators asked him to draw a detailed map of the area where he claimed to have witnessed the shooting. His interrogation was long and searching, and he was made to repeat the story many times. In essential details, it did not change. French occupants of nearby buildings were the next to be interrogated, and they reported the presence of uneven earth in the garden. Eighteen bodies of Canadian soldiers were discovered, buried in five different graves.

The questioning of Kurt Meyer in London was conducted largely by Colonel Alexander Scotland. A formidable interrogator, he spoke perfect German, and his assessment of Meyer was succinct:

'A bully of a commander… He was the voice which in the beer garden always rose above everyone else's.

I had met many such. Nor was it difficult to imagine how it was that the aggressive Meyer, active… self-possessed… had so rapidly advanced from the rank of Captain to Lieutenant General in the space of a few years.'

Evidence of Meyer's complicity in the murders was deemed sufficient to have him returned to Germany to face charges as a war criminal. On arrival, he saluted the knot of assembled Canadians, a gesture they ignored. In the presence of a colonel of the 4th Winnipeg Rifles, the charges were read to him:

1. That in Belgium in 1943 and in France 1944, as a commander of the 25th SS Panzer Grenadier Regiment, he had ordered the troops under his command to show no mercy to Allied troops.

2. That he, Meyer, had committed a war crime in Normandy in that as Commander of the 25th SS Panzer Grenadier Regiment he was responsible for the murder of seven Canadian prisoners near his HQ.

The evidence against Meyer certainly appeared damning, particularly when Captain Percy Bell of the Canadian Graves Unit reported that exhumation of the bodies had revealed death being due to wounds to the head, caused either from bullets or a blunt instrument such as a club or rifle butt. At first, Meyer refused to admit even the scantiest knowledge of the murders. However, in the time that lapsed between his interrogation by the Canadians and the trial, he had second thoughts, admitting to the court that two officers did report to him that they had found the unburied bodies of Canadians, who had been shot in the area of Abbaye Ardenne. He testified:

'I sent my adjutant, *Oberscharführer* Schuman, to investigate. He confirmed the report and I went over myself to make the inspection. All the Canadians had been shot through the head. I then reported the matter to my divisional commander, *SS-Brigadeführer* Witt, who was very angry and asked me to discover who was responsible.'

Meyer had then ordered the prisoners to be buried and an investigation carried out. But the death of Fritz Witt intervened, Meyer was promoted, and no action

Above: Propaganda Minister Josef Göbbels awards Hugo Kraas, later the final commander of the *Hitlerjugend* Division, his Knight's Cross in April 1943 after the Battle of Kharkov. On Kraas's right is Max Wünsche.

was taken. At the final session of the trial, the verdict was read out:

'Kurt Meyer, this Court has found you guilty on three counts. You are sentenced to death by shooting.'

There were those, however, who felt that the verdict was unjust, since no clear evidence existed that Meyer had actually ordered the killings. The authorities remained uneasy, and the sentence was commuted to life imprisonment. In 1951, Meyer was sent back to Germany from a Canadian prison. On 7 September 1954, he was finally released, having served 10 years.

The remainder of his life was devoted to the welfare of former *SS* men through HIAG, the *Waffen-SS* Old Comrades' Association. He was careful to urge that

HIAG should be entirely an ex-serviceman's organization and should have no connection with neo-Nazi organizations. Kurt Meyer died of a heart attack on 23 December 1961, having published *Grenadiere*, a somewhat lurid account of his wartime role, whose accuracy was challenged by many.

HUBERT MEYER

Unlike many of his fellow *Waffen-SS* adherents, Hubert Meyer, a Berliner who was to have a brief tenure as commander of the *Hitlerjugend* Division in succession to Kurt Meyer (no relation), had not intended to follow a career in the army. At school he studied chemistry and had passed the basic exam in 1934 when he was 21 years old. By then, however, he had been attracted to the career opportunities offered by the *SS-Verfügungstruppen* (SS-VT), and the next year joined 12 Company of the *Deutschland* Regiment. In 1936, Meyer was chosen to attend the third cadet course at

Junkerschule Bad Tolz. After graduation he undertook a course for platoon leaders, and was commissioned on 20 April 1937 with the rank of *SS-Untersturmführer*. That same year he was given command of a platoon with the 10th Company of the *Leibstandarte*.

Meyer saw service in Poland, where he earned the Iron Cross Second Class and also served as Adjutant to *Leibstandarte*'s 3rd Battalion during the battles in Holland and France. He was commander of 12th Company throughout the Balkan campaign, where he won the Iron Cross First Class on 7 July 1941, and held this command throughout the opening weeks of Operation Barbarossa, particularly in the bid to surround Uman. The Company came up against a detachment of well-concealed enemy snipers and engaged in hand-to-hand fighting to reach their objectives. Meyer was severely wounded in the ensuing mêlée and spent the next three months on sick leave. During the winter of 1941–1942, Meyer was posted to the *Leibstandarte*'s Artillery Regiment for General Staff training, and during March of that year was awarded the Infantry Assault Badge in Bronze.

While leading a counter-attack south of Kharkov, Hubert Meyer, now promoted to the rank of *SS-Hauptsturmführer*, was wounded yet again, which led to him receiving the German Cross in Gold with immediate promotion to *SS-Sturmbannführer*. With his graduation following the General Staff Officer course, he was appointed to 12th SS Panzer Division *Hitlerjugend*. When the division's commander, *Brigadeführer* Kurt Meyer, was taken prisoner, Hubert Meyer took over temporary command of the division with the relatively junior rank of *SS-Obersturmbannführer*, until the brief tenure of Fritz Krämer, which in turn was followed by that of the final commander, Hugo Kraas. He remained the division's chief of staff for the rest of the war and surrendered to the Americans with the rest of the division on 8 May 1945.

Still alive at the time of writing, Hubert Meyer has remained one of the most lively and active members of the former division. An unabashed apologist for the *Waffen-SS* generally, whom he has consistently claimed were 'soldiers just like the others', he attracted considerable opposition to his visit to Britain in the 1970s

when he publicised a book on the units' fighting record. He is the author of the immensely detailed *The History of SS Panzer Division Hitlerjugend*, and has made himself readily accessible over the years to advise war historians and film makers.

After retirement from the Aga Gavaert photographic company, Hubert Meyer became a prominent speaker in the HIAG, the ex-servicemen's association for former members of the *Waffen-SS*.

FRITZ KRÄMER

SS-Brigadeführer Fritz Krämer, who was briefly in command of 12th SS Panzer Division *Hitlerjugend*, was an unusual member of the *Waffen-SS* in that he served in the *Wehrmacht* until January 1943. Then he was transferred on loan to I SS Panzer Corps, where he was selected by Sepp Dietrich to be his senior administrative officer.

Born on 12 December 1900 in Stettin, Krämer entered the German Army straight from school, but left to join the Prussian police force, on whose strength he remained until October 1934. Finally opting for a full-time military career, Krämer rejoined the *Wehrmacht* with the rank of *Oberleutnant*. He graduated from the Berlin War Academy in May 1935 and by the following year was appointed commander of an infantry regimental company. At the outbreak of World War II, he was sent, as a member of 13th Infantry Division (Motorized), to Poland. Later, he gained the Iron Cross First Class for his actions in France.

With 13th Panzer Division, Krämer served in Russia, where he was awarded the German Cross in Gold and the Knights Cross. Sepp Dietrich, always a keen talent spotter, made a wise choice when he selected Krämer as his senior administrative officer. Krämer had a solid and comprehensive staff background, was an experienced officer and had just what Dietrich needed to help him with the complexities of running a corps. But he was still only on loan from the *Wehrmacht*, even though he was given what amounted to the honorary rank of *SS-Oberführer*. Indeed, it was not until the start of August 1944 that he became an *SS-Brigadeführer* and was an 'official' SS man. Throughout the rest of his career, he was seldom absent from Dietrich's side and was trusted absolutely by his commander for whom, during the battles in Normandy, he at times deputized. On 24 October, he succeeded Hubert Meyer as commander of the *Hitlerjugend* Division – Hubert Meyer having held the post for two months after Kurt Meyer's capture. But he was not to have the job for long and was soon transferred to the reserve, his place being taken by Hugo Kraas. For the remainder of the war, he served with Dietrich's Sixth SS Panzer Army.

On surrendering to the Americans, he was arraigned, along with Sepp Dietrich, as a war criminal for his part in the murder of 83 American prisoners at the Malmédy crossroads in Normandy in December 1944. He was tried at Dachau in 1946 and received a sentence of 10 years' imprisonment. Following his release and until his death on 23 June 1959, Fritz Krämer lived in Hoxter, Germany. His funeral was attended by many of his former comrades.

HUGO KRAAS

Hugo Kraas, who took over command of 12th SS-Panzer Divsion *Hitlerjugend* from Fritz Krämer, was born in the Ruhr on 25 January 1911. The eldest of seven sons, he had originally intended to become a teacher, but the death of his father left the family fortunes severely depleted. His schooling was cut short and he was obliged to seek work. At the age of 21, he became a member of the National Socialist Party, subsequently joining the *Sturm Abteilung* (the Brownshirts of the SA) followed by brief service in the army. He soon realized that the growth of the SS, particularly the *SS-Verfügungstruppe* (itself the forerunner of the *Waffen-SS*), offered the choicest opportunities to ambitious young men. He joined the *Germania* Regiment with the rank of *SS-Rottenführer*, attending the elite *Braunschweig SS Junkerschule*, graduating second in his class and earning promotion to *SS-Untersturmführer*.

He was assigned to the *Leibstandarte Adolf Hitler*. As the Führer's bodyguard, this was considered the elite of the SS formations. Kraas was given command of a platoon with *14 Panzerjagerkompanie* (anti-tank), under the command of Kurt Meyer, the future commander of 12th SS Panzer Division *Hitlerjugend*. The platoon took part in the invasion of Poland, and Kraas was

Right: Max Wünsche (with a head wound) astride a motorcycle combination with Rudolf von Ribbentrop, son of the German Foreign Minister and commander of 3rd Company, 12th SS Panzer Regiment, on 9 June 1944.

awarded the Iron Cross Second Class. Some idea of the impression he made on Kurt Meyer can be judged by the fact that Meyer, when given command of *15 Kradschutzenkompanie* (Motor Cycle) in November 1939, chose Hugo Kraas as his sole platoon leader. With Kraas's progression to *SS-Obersturmführer* came command of the second platoon for the invasion of Holland, where he became the first officer of the *Leibstandarte* to be awarded the Iron Cross First Class. In what was regarded as something of a coup, Kraas had advanced some 80km (50 miles) beyond the Issel river, capturing 127 prisoners.

The invasion of Holland and France meant that his platoon was enlarged to a company, of which he assumed command. Kraas was at Meyer's side in the Balkans and in the Soviet Union, where he made a particular mark in the battles of Rostov. The increasing prestige of the *Leibstandarte*, which was reorganized in June 1942 as a Panzer Grenadier Division, was mirrored by Kraas's own career – in command of a battalion, he led his forces first throughout the retreat and then the triumphant reconquest of Kharkov in March 1943. The award of the Knight's Cross was followed by further promotion, and he became comamnder of 2nd SS Panzer Grenadier Regiment, with the rank of *SS-Obersturmbannführer*, shortly before the Battle of Kursk, codenamed Operation Zitadelle, in July 1943.

The regiment was given the daunting task of capturing the key objective of the heavily bunkered Hill 234, lying beyond the town of Bykova. It was here that Kraas encountered the greatest opposition and some of the toughest fighting of his career. The assault began at 4a.m., but soon ground to a snail's pace under furious Soviet bombardment, taking heavy casualties. Kraas rallied his remaining forces, which were reorganized into three assault groups and succeeded in breaking through, breasting the hill and weakening Soviet resistance after further heavy combat. But Operation Zitadelle itself was doomed to failure:

following the Allied landings in Sicily, it was called off in August 1943.

The debacle at Kursk presaged the general weakening of German power on the Eastern Front. Nonetheless, 2nd SS Panzer Grenadier Regiment stood firm, defending the division's left flank against an assault by some 90 T-34s, carrying four regiments of infantry attacking from the north and south. Kraas was able to halt the advance by establishing a new front line in the Soviets' assembly area, thus preventing encirclement. But retreat was only a matter of time and the regiment fell back to the village of Voroschino, which the Soviets intended to encircle. In four days of defensive action, Kraas was able to deplete much of the Soviet spearhead before the withdrawal resumed.

Kraas was wounded on 5 January 1944. He was obliged to step down from his command, but received the consolation of an award of Oak Leaves to his Knight's Cross for gallantry at Kursk and Zhitomir, together with elevation in rank to *SS-Standartenführer*. On recovery, he attended a divisional commanders' course before transfer to 12th SS Panzer Division *Hitlerjugend,* succeeding Fritz Krämer as the last commander and reaching the rank of *SS-Brigadeführer und Generalmajor der Waffen-SS.* The campaign in the Ardennes, most notably the assault with heavy infantry support on Butgenbach, cost the *Hitlerjugend* dear, as did the later campaign in Hungary, east of Lake Balaton, where it formed part of Sixth SS Panzer Army, and aimed to recapture Budapest. The division was forced to retreat. On 8 May 1945 the survivors crossed the Allied boundary demarcation line at the Enns river near Linz in Austria, surrendering to the forces of the American Seventh Army.

Hugo Kraas was held as a prisoner of war until 1948. During that time he was accused of involvement in the massacre of American troops by men of the *Waffen-SS* on 17 December 1944. Surviving members of *Kampfgruppe Peiper,* including Peiper himself, of the *Leibstandarte* Division, were also arrested and put on trial. An affidavit was sworn by Rudolf Sauer, formerly of the *Hitlerjugend* Division, that Kraas was present and had given an order that no prisoners were to be taken.

Kraas was sentenced to three years' imprisonment. He died of a heart attack in Seik, Schlewig-Holstein on 20 February 1980.

MAX WÜNSCHE

A resourceful and courageous young officer, Max Wünsche had an outstanding career in the *Waffen-SS.* Born on 20 April 1914 at Kittlitz near Lobau, he joined the *SS-Verfügungstruppe* at the age of 20, as SS No 153508. His potential was swiftly realized and he was sent to *SS Junkerschule Bad Tolz,* becoming an *SS-Untersturmführer* on his birthday in 1936. After some service in the *Leibstandarte,* he was appointed an aide-de-camp to Hitler, accompanying the Führer to Poland. But he was determined on a military career, which brought the prospects of promotion, and on his return to his unit was sent to command a company in France. During the brief campaign there, he was wounded and was awarded both classes of the Iron Cross.

In the Balkans, his efficiency and energy led to him serving in the demanding position of Adjutant to Sepp Dietrich, with the rank of *SS-Hauptsturmführer.* With the launch of the invasion of Russia, he was attached to Army Group South and General Eberherd von Mackesen's III Corps. His division faced bitter resistance during the early days of the invasion, but by July the *Leibstandarte* was able to advance at speed. A great believer in reconnaissance, Wünsche on numerous occasions took a Fieseler Storch aircraft and flew over enemy-held territory, Although many of these flights were regarded by his comrades as reckless, they proved their worth, facilitating the capture of Nov-Archelsk. This, in turn, closed the Uman pocket and sealed the fates of the trapped Soviet divisions.

After the command of an Assault Gun Detachment in Russia, he was sent to the War Academy, from which he emerged in late 1942 to take command of the

newly formed 1st Battalion of the 1st SS Panzer Regiment in the capacity of *SS-Sturmbannführer.* The excellence of his service earned him the German Cross in Gold and, on 28th February 1943, his Knight's Cross, as well as further promotion to *SS-Obersturmbannführer.* In July 1943, along with other conspicuous talents from the *Leibstandarte,* Wünsche was transferred to 12th SS Division *Hitlerjugend,* where, at the age of 28, he became commander of the 12th SS Panzer Regiment.

On 6 June 1944, the Allies hit the beaches of Normandy and consolidated their beachhead preparatory to the deep push inland. British and Canadian forces then ran directly into the forces of the division. In the ensuing battle, Wünsche and his regiment were credited with destroying 219 enemy tanks in eight weeks, a figure later revised upwards to 250 tanks. For his resolute leadership, Wünsche was awarded Oak Leaves to the Knight's Cross on 11 August 1944.

On the night of 20 August, Wünsche, his adjutant *SS-Haupsturmführer* Isecke, *SS-Untersturmführer* Freitag and a wounded medical officer made good their escape from the Falaise pocket. During their travels on foot, they encountered an enemy outpost, where the injured doctor was taken prisoner and Wünsche received injuries to his calf. Subsequently, Isecke, who had become separated, was also captured. Wünsche and Freitag were now on their own and, by luck, found a German vehicle that was in good working order. With considerable panache, the two men drove through the town of St Lambert in full view of the occupying Canadians. But by then Wünsche's wound was giving him trouble, and the pair took refuge in a clump of bushes to await darkness. There they were eventually spotted and captured.

Wünsche survived the war, becoming the manager of an industrial plant in Wuppertal. He died in Munich on 17th April 1995, aged 85.

Right: *SS-Obersturmbannführer* **Max Wünsche, seen here aboard a tank on the Normandy front, where his 12th SS Panzer Regiment succeeded in destroying 250 enemy tanks in eight weeks.**

DIVISIONAL COMMANDERS

24.6.43–14.6.44
Brigadeführer **Fritz de Witt**

24.10.44–11.13.44
Brigadeführer **Fritz Kraemer**

14.6.44–6.9.44
Brigadeführer **Kurt Meyer**

13.11.44–8.5.45
Brigadeführer **Hugo Kraas**

6.9.4 –24.10.44
Obersturmbannführer **Hubert Meyer**

WAFFEN-SS RANKS AND THEIR ENGLISH EQUIVALENTS

SS-Schütze	Private	**SS-Hauptsturmführer**	Captain
SS-Oberschütze	Senior Private, attained	**SS-Sturmbannführer**	Major
	after six months' service	**SS-Oberbannsturmführer**	Lieutenant-Colonel
SS-Sturmmann	Lance-Corporal	**SS-Standartenführer**	Colonel
SS-Rottenführer	Corporal	**SS-Oberführer**	Senior Colonel
SS-Unterscharführer	Senior Corporal	**SS-Brigadeführer**	Major-General
	/Lance-Sergeant	**und Generalmajor der Waffen-SS**	
SS-Scharführer	Sergeant	**SS-Gruppenführer und**	Lieutenant-General
SS-Oberscharführer	Staff Sergeant	**Generalleutnant der Waffen-SS**	
SS-Hauptscharführer	Warrant Officer	**SS-Obergruppenführer**	General
SS-Sturmscharführer	Senior Warrant Officer	**und General der Waffen-SS**	
	after 15 years' service	**SS-Oberstgruppenführer**	Colonel-General
SS-Untersturmführer	Second Lieutenant	**und Generaloberst der Waffen-SS**	
SS-Obersturmführer	First Lieutenant	**Reichsführer-SS**	(no English equivalent)

WAR SERVICE

Date	Corps	Army	Army Group	Area
8.43 – 4.44	Forming	–	D	Antwerp
5.44	Reserve	–	OKW	Evreux
6.44	I SS	7th Army	B	Evreux
7.44	LXXXVI	Panzergruppe West	B	Normandy
8.44	LXXX	1st Army	B	Loire
9.44 (kgr.)	I SS	7th Army	B	Eifel
10.44 (remnants)	LXVI	7th Army	B	Eifel
11.44	refitting	BdE	–	Bremen
12.44	Reserve	6th Pz. Army	OB West	Eifel
1.45	Reserve	5th Pz. Army	B	Ardennes
2.45	Feldherrnhalle (IV)	8th Army	South	Hungary
3.45	Reserve	–	South	Hungary
4.45	I SS	6th Pz. Army	South	Hungary
5.45	Reserve	6th Pz. Army	Ostmark	Austria

ORDER OF BATTLE MAY 1944

Divisionsbegleit Company
SS-Obersturmführer Fritz Guntrum
SS-Obersturmführer Erwin StIer
I.Zug - Schützen
II.Zug - s.M.G
III.Zug - Pak
IV.Zug - Flak
V.Zug - le.I.G
VI.Zug - Kradschützen

SS-Panzer Regiment 12
SS-Obersturmbannführer Max Wünsche Captured:
24.8.44
SS-Sturmbannführer Herbert Kuhlman
SS-Obersturmbannführer Martin Gross

I. Panzerabteilung
SS-Sturmbannführer Arnold Jürgensen Died: 23.12.44
SS-Hauptsturmführer Rudolf Von Ribbentrop
1. Company - SS-Hauptsturmführer Kurt Anton Berlin
2. Company - SS-Oberstumführer Helmut Gaede
3. Company - SS-Obersturmführer Rudolf Von
Ribbentrop
4. Company - SS-Hauptsturmführer Hans Pfeiffer
Repair Company - SS-Untersturmführer Robert Maier

II. Panzerabteilung
SS-Sturmbannführer Karl-Heinz Prinz Died: 14.8.44
SS-Sturmbannführer Hans Siegel Erfasst: 20.4.45
5. Company - SS-Obersturmführer Helmut Bando
6. Company - SS-Hauptsturmführer Ludwig Ruckdeschel
7. Company - SS-Hauptsturmführer Patrick Rösen
8. Company - SS-Obersturmführer Hans Siegel
9. Company - SS-Obersturmführer Ostuf Buettner
Repair Company - SS-Hauptsturmführer Karl Müller

SS-Panzergrenadier Regiment 25
SS-Standartenführer Kurt Meyer Until: 14.6.44
SS-Obersturmbannführer Karl-Heinz Milius
SS-Sturmbannführer Siegfried Müller

I. Battalion
SS-Sturmbannführer Hans Waldmüller Died: 8.9.44
SS-Hauptsturmführer Alfons Ott
1. Company
2. Company
3. Company
4 Company

II. Battalion
SS-Sturmbannführer Hans Scappini Died: 7.6.44
SS-Hauptsturmführer Heinz Schrott Died: 2.9.44
SS-Obersturmbannführer Richard Schulze

5. Company
6. Company
7. Company
8. Company

III. Battalion
SS-Sturmbannführer Karl-Heinz Milius
SS-Hauptsturmführer Alfred Brückner
SS-Hauptsturmführer Wilhelm Dehne
9. Company
10. Company
11. Company
12. Company
13. Company
14. Company
15. Company
16. Company

SS-Panzergrenadier Regiment 26
SS-Obersturmbannführer Wilhelm Mohnke
SS-Obersturmbannführer Bernhard Krause Died: 19.2.45

I. Battalion
SS-Sturmbannführer Berhard Krause
SS-Hauptsturmführer Gerd Hein
SS-Sturmbannführer Erich Kostenbader Died: 8.3.45
1. Company
2. Company
3. Company
4. Company

II. Battalion
SS-Sturmbannführer Bernhard Siebken
SS-Hauptsturmführer Karl Hauschild
5. Company
6. Company
7. Company
8. Company

III. Battalion
SS-Sturmbannführer Erich Olboeter Died: 2.9.44
SS-Hauptsturmführer Georg Urabl From: 23.9.44
SS-Hauptsturmführer Hermann Brand
9. Company
10. Company
11. Company
12. Company
13. Company
14. Company
15. Company
16. Company

SS-Panzeraufklärungsabteilung 12
SS-Sturmbannführer Gerd Bremer
1. Company
2. Company
3. Company
4. Company
5. Company

SS-Panzerjägerabteilung 12
SS-Sturmbannführer Jakob Hanreich
SS-Sturmbannführer Karl-Heinz Brockschmidt
1. Company - SS-Obersturmführer Georg Hurdlebrink
2. Company - SS-Obersturmführer Wachter
3. Company - SS-Hauptsturmführer Wöst

SS-Panzer Artillery Regiment 12
SS-Obersturmbannführer Fritz Schröder
SS-Obersturmbannführer Oskar Drexler

I. Abteilung
SS-Sturmbannführer Eric Urbanitz
SS-Sturmbannführer Karl Müller
1. Battery
2. Battery
3. Battery

II. Abteilung
SS-Sturmbannführer Alfred Schöps Died: 6.27.44
SS-Sturmbannführer Günter Neumann
4. Battery
5. Battery
6. Battery

III. Abteilung
SS-Sturmbannführer Karl Bartling
SS-Sturmbannführer Fritsch
7. Battery
8. Battery
9. Battery
10. Battery

SS-Werferabteilung 12
SS-Sturmbannführer Willy Müller
SS-Hauptsturmführer Ziesenitz
1. Battery
2. Battery
3. Battery
4. Battery

SS-Flakabteilung 12
SS-Sturmbannführer Rudolph Fend
SS-Sturmbannführer Dr. Wolfgang Loenicker
1. Battery

2. Battery
3. Battery
4. Battery
5. Battery

SS-Panzer Pioneer Battalion 12
SS-Sturmbannführer Siegfried Müller
SS-Sturmbannführer Johannes Taubert
1. Company
2. Company
3. Company
4. Company

SS-Panzernachrichtenabteilung 12
SS-Sturmbannführer Erich Pandel
SS-Hauptsturmführer Krüger
1. Company
2. Company

Die Versorgungstruppen

SS-Nachschubtruppen 12
SS-Sturmbannführer Rolf Kolitz
1. Company
2. Company
3. Company
4. Company
5. Company
6. Company

SS-Instandsetzungsabteilung 12
SS-Sturmbannführer Artur Manthei
1. Company
2. Company
3. Company
4. Company
5. Company

SS-Wirtschaftsbataillon 12
SS-Sturmbannführer Dr. Kos
SS-Hauptsturmführer Günther Reichenbach
Bäckerei Company
Schlächterei Company
Verpflegungsamt
Feldpostamt

SS-Sanitätsabteilung 12
SS-Standartenführer Rolf Schulz
Sanitäts Company
Sanitäts Company
Krakenkraftwagen Company
Versorgungs Company

WAFFEN-SS DIVISIONS 1939–45

Title (and nominal divisional strength at the beginning of 1945)	Granted Divisional Status	Knight's Crosses Awarded
1st SS-Panzer Division *Leibstandarte-SS Adolf Hitler* (22,000)	1942	58
2nd SS-Panzer Division *Das Reich* (18,000)	1939	69
3rd SS-Panzer Division *Totenkopf* (15,400)	1939	47
4th SS-Panzergrenadier Division *Polizei* (9,000)	1939	25
5th SS-Panzer Division *Wiking* (14,800)	1940	55
6th SS-Gebirgs Division *Nord* (15,000)	1941	4
7th SS-Freiwilligen Gebirgs Division *Prinz Eugen* (20,000)	1942	6
8th SS-Kavallerie Division *Florian Geyer* (13,000)	1942	22
9th SS-Panzer Division *Hohenstaufen* (19,000)	1943	12
10th SS-Panzer Division *Frundsberg* (15,500)	1943	13
11th SS-Freiwilligen Panzergrenadier Division *Nordland* (9,000)	1943	25
12th SS-Panzer Division *Hitlerjugend* (19,500)	1943	14
13th Waffen Gebirgs Division der SS *Handschar* (12,700)	1943	4
14th Waffen Grenadier Division der SS (22,000)	1943	1
15th Waffen Grenadier Division der SS (16,800)	1943	3
16th SS-Panzergrenadier Division *Reichsführer-SS* (14,000)	1943	1
17th SS-Panzergrenadier Division *Götz von Berlichingen* (3500)	1943	4
18th SS-Freiwilligen Panzergrenadier Division *Horst Wessel* (11,000)	1944	2
19th Waffen Grenadier Division der SS (9000)	1944	12
20th Waffen Grenadier Division der SS (15,500)	1944	5
21st Waffen Gebirgs Division der SS *Skanderbeg* (5000)	1944	0
22nd SS-Freiwilligen Kavallerie Division *Maria Theresa* (8000)	1944	6
23rd Waffen Gebirgs Division der SS *Kama* (disbanded late 1944, number '23' given to next division)	1944	0
23rd SS-Freiwilligen Panzergrenadier Division *Nederland* (6000)	1945	19
24th Waffen Gebirgskarstjäger Division der SS (3000)	1944	0
25th Waffen Grenadier Division der SS *Hunyadi* (15,000)	1944	0
26th Waffen Grenadier Division der SS (13,000)	1945	0
27th SS-Freiwilligen Grenadier Division *Langemarck* (7000)	1944	1
28th SS-Freiwilligen Grenadier Division *Wallonien* (4000)	1944	3
29th Waffen Grenadier Division der SS (disbanded late 1944, number '29' given to next division)	1944	0
29th Waffen Grenadier Division der SS (15,000)	1945	0
30th Waffen Grenadier Division der SS (4500)	1945	0

31st SS-Freiwilligen Grenadier Division *Böhmen-Mähren* (11,000)	1945	0
32nd SS-Freiwilligen Grenadier Division *30 Januar* (2000)	1945	0
33rd Waffen *Kavallerie* Division der SS (destroyed soon after formation, number '33' given to next division)	1945	0
33rd Waffen Grenadier Division der SS *Charlemagne* (7000)	1945	2
34th SS-Freiwilligen Grenadier Division *Landstorm Nederland* (7000)	1945	3
35th SS-Polizei Grenadier Division (5000)	1945	0
36th Waffen Grenadier Division der SS (6000)	1945	1
37th SS-Freiwilligen Kavallerie Division *Lützow* (1000)	1945	0
38th SS-Grenadier Division *Nibelungen* (1000)	1945	0

BIBLIOGRAPHY

Butler, Rupert, *Hitler's Young Tigers*, Arrow Books, 1986.

Crookenden, Lt Gen Sir Napier, *Battle of the Bulge*, Ian Allan Ltd, 1980.

Cross, Robin, *Fallen Eagle: The Last Days of the Third Reich*, Michael O'Mara Books Ltd, 1993.

Leigh Davis, Brian, *Badges and Insignia of the Third Reich 1933-1945*, Blandford Press, 1983.

Hastings, Max, *Overlord: D-Day and the Battle for Normandy 1944*, Michael Joseph, 1984.

Knopp, Guido, *Hitler's Children,* Sutton Publishing, 2000.

Kessler, Leo, *SS Peiper*, Leo Cooper, in association with Secker & Warburg, Ltd, 1986.

Keegan, John, *Six Armies in Normandy,* Jonathan Cape, 1982.

Koch, H W, *The Hitler Youth, Origins and Development 1922-1945*, Macdonald & Jane's, 1975.

Lucas, James, and Barker, James, *The Killing Ground: The Battle of Falaise Gap, August 1944,* Batsford, 1978.

Maschmann, Melita, *Account Rendered, A dossier of my former self*, Aberlard Schumann, 1964.

Maule, Henry, *Caen, The Brutal Battle and Break-out from Normandy*, Purnell Book Services, 1976.

McDonald, Charles, *The Battle of the Bulge*, Weidenfeld & Nicholson, 1984.

Messenger, Charles, *The Last Prussian: A Biography of Field Marshal Gerd von Rundstedt, 1875–1953*, Brasseys, 1991.

Meyer, Hubert, *The History of the 12th SS Panzer Division, Hitler Jugend*, Federowicz Publishers, 1994

Meyer, Kurt, *Grenadiere*, Schild Verlag, 1957.

Parker, Danny S, *Battle of the Bulge: Hitler's Ardennes Offensive 1944-1945*, Greenhill Books, 1991.

Neave, Airey, *Nuremberg, A Personal Record of the Trial of the Major Nazi War Criminals*, Coronet Books, 1978.

Reader's Digest Illustrated History of World War II, The Reader's Digest, 1989.

Reitlinger, Gerald, *The SS Alibi of a Nation*, William Heinemann, 1956.

Rempel, Gerhard, *Hitler's Children: The Hitler Youth and the SS*, The University of North Caroline Press, 1989.

Reynolds, Michael, *The Devil's Adjutant, Jochen Peiper, Panzer Leader*, Spellmount, 1997

Stein, George S, *The Waffen-SS: Hitler's Elite Guard at War 1939–1945*, Cornell University Press, 1996.

Von Schirach, Henrietta, *The Price of Glory*, Frederick Muller, 1960.

Toland, John, *The Last 100 Days*, Arthur Barker, 1965.

Trevor-Roper, H R, *The Last Days of Hitler*, (Revised Edition), Macmillan, 1972.

INDEX